NFER Publishing Company

Reading tests in the classroom

Vincent & Cresswell

Reading Tests in the Classroom

Denis Vincent and Michael Cresswell

NFER Publishing Company Ltd

Published by the NFER Publishing Company Ltd.,
2 Jennings Buildings, Thames Avenue,
Windsor, Berks. SL4 1QS
Registered Office: The Mere, Upton Park, Slough SL1 2DQ
First published 1976
© D. Vincent and M. Cresswell
ISBN 0 85633 101 5

Typeset by Jubal Multiwrite Ltd.,
66 Loampit Vale, London SE13 7SN
Printed in Great Britain by
John Gardner (Printers) Ltd.,
Hawthorne Road, Bootle, Merseyside, L20 6JX
Distributed in the USA by Humanities Press Inc.,
Hillary House—Fernhill House, Atlantic Highlands,
New Jersey 07716 USA.

Contents

ACKNOWLEDGEMENTS

The authors wish to thank colleagues, both within and outside the NFER who have assisted them in the production of this book.

In particular we are indebted to David Moseley, Betty Root, M. Purushothaman and June Derrick who commented so fully and constructively on early versions, although we are only too conscious that in places we may have failed to rectify some of the shortcomings they pointed out.

Much of the material in Chapters Two and Three was developed through trials (and errors!) with teachers attending in-service courses on testing. In this respect we are particularly grateful to those who attended courses at Dyffryn and Stoke in 1975. In addition the content of the book in general owes much to the questions, comments and problems of teachers who have attended NFER courses and talks on educational testing in the past few years or who individually sought the help of the NFER's Guidance and Assessment Service.

We also wish to thank Kath Bradley, Carol Vile, Ray Sumner and Judy Dean for their support and their comments on individual chapters. Finally, thanks to Arnold Kanarek for his relentless encouragement throughout the writing of this book and to Dianne Horton for her patient preparation of the final typescript.

D.R.V.
M.J.C.
January 1976

INTRODUCTION

This book is intended for reading teachers who wish to add a knowledge of standardized testing to their body of teaching skills.

While it is possible to find a wide range of texts on the teaching of reading *or* about educational testing, very few have managed to combine the two topics. As a consequence many teachers of reading lack the knowledge, critical understanding and confidence to make informed selection and use of reading tests.

The present book is an attempt to remedy this deficit by providing a discussion of the key issues in educational testing in terms directly relevant to the teaching of reading.

Tests do not tell the teacher how to teach reading and nor does this book. While we have tried to keep our discussion of reading itself at a non-technical level it is to be hoped that teachers will appreciate that a sound background in teaching reading is essential if any constructive use is to be made of reading tests.

Substantial space has been given to the technical or 'psychometric' aspects of reading testing. From experience we know that many teachers are unfamiliar with this aspect of testing and that some of the concepts involved are found difficult to comprehend. Many people find a simple explanation or a single text insufficient for a complete understanding to be reached. We recommend that our own chapters be read as an introduction to the subject — as a sample of the kind of thinking behind much educational testing — and that the reader be prepared to consult further texts if necessary.

Limitations

At the centre of much of this technical material is the notion of test-error. This is the characteristic of tests to provide an estimate — a highly 'scientific' guess — of how well a child can read, rather than to measure some kind of fixed quantity which is 'within' the reader. The point is that even the best tests can only be an inexact guide to reading ability. Properly interpreted their results can be useful — although so can many other ways of observing and studying a child's reading. They are thus an additional and perhaps ancilliary teaching technique and should never be allowed to become a dominant influence in the classroom. Misinterpreted they can be positively harmful. To a naive teacher or parent the news that a child 'has been tested' and that he has got a score of such and such can have a tone of absolute truth and finality which leaves them with a complete and far-reaching misconception about the child, how he is to be taught and what is to be expected of him.

While this is very much a book about how to use and interpret tests we have felt it necessary to digress occasionally into some of the ideological arguments about the pros and cons of testing. While we are convinced that tests can be used constructively in teaching reading we are only too aware that the use of such powerful tools requires a lively sense of the philosophical and practical arguments which take place about testing. In particular we feel that many of the arguments made against testing revolve around the possibility of misuse and misinterpretation in ignorant hands and that many of the dangers of testing are virtually eliminated once the limitations are understood. At the present time much reading testing is carried out by teachers who have had no special training or knowledge in educational testing, and many of the objections to the use of tests arise from this cause, rather than from any intrinsic perversity of the tests themselves. Incidentally, this book does not argue for more use of reading tests, but for a more judicious approach where they are used.

Reading ability, attainment and achievement

Some explanation of terms should be made at this point. The terms 'ability', 'attainment' and 'achievement' seem to be used in an interchangeable way with reference to reading, although in testing terms they mean two different things. A person's 'ability' is usually taken to simply mean the amount of skill or proficiency he possesses. The terms 'attainment' and 'achievement' are synonymous, but refer to how much a person has actually *learned*, how far he has progressed in acquiring skill or knowledge. The term 'ability' leaves unanswered the question as to *how* knowledge was acquired; formal learning, incidental learning or innate capacity are all possibilities. In reading the first two processes are both important. Most early reading skill is acquired as a result of teaching — it is thus reasonable to speak of reading achievement here. However later, and at a point not easily defined, the pupil is often left to develop reading skill on his own, mainly through sheer practice. His reading ability is thus now more a result of his capacity to learn for himself. It is probably still fair to speak of it as attainment and achievement, even though we now mean something different. In general the distinction between ability and attainment is not crucial for following the discussion in this book and little of the sense will be lost if the reader regards them as meaning the same thing: the capacity to read.

Reading skill and reading process

These two terms are used differently. Reading is a 'skill' because it is something children have to learn to *do*. Like most skills it is acquired to a varying extent, like proficiency in driving a car, operating a lathe or throwing a dart. When we refer to reading skill, we mean the proficiency that the child displays in performing a particular task. Often reference will be made to component skills or reading sub-skills. These are also activities which can be performed with varying degrees of proficiency. Each sub-skill is a single part or strand of reading. One on its own could not be described as 'reading', but where sub-skills are patterned, co-ordinated and used together they go to make up the skill of reading proper.

When we refer to the reading 'process' we wish to refer to all the activities which go on when someone reads — all the physiological and psychological events that must take place — regardless of the degree of ability or skill the reader exhibits. This includes the performance of the sub-skills, together with much other activity about which we can only speculate.

The most concise way the relationship between these terms can be expressed is to say that a reading test evokes a child's reading *skill* (the *performance* of a specified task) in order to assess his *ability* or *attainment* and that it is in performance of the test task that the reading process takes place.

Reading and other language skills

Most teachers who are concerned with reading will be equally interested in all other aspects of language and where possible we have discussed assessment in language generally. We have concentrated on reading however because this is the area where most testing does actually take place and for which most published tests exist. Further, at the present time much less is known about what is involved in teaching other language skills, and similarly very much less expertise exists in testing these skills. It is certainly by no means clear that the methods developed for reading testing would be appropriate for assessment in other areas.

Who is authorized to use tests?

The question of who may use tests in schools is of sufficient importance to need mention at the outset for regardless of whether they are desirable tools or not, they are certainly powerful ones. We therefore recommend that no standardized tests (see following chapters for a definition of these) are used in school without the knowledge of a senior member of staff. It is also desirable for this condition to be observed where any published test materials are to be used, even if they are unstandardized.

Most schools' psychological services employ standardized or other published test materials. Prior consultation with such agencies should take place to ensure that the school's testing programme does not conflict with or duplicate that carried out by the psychologists, or indeed by the local educational authority.

Test publishers impose restrictions on the sale of their tests to prevent their use by unsuitable persons. Few educational tests are supplied directly to bookshops for example, and publishers may supply only to senior teachers or to persons with recognized qualifications. The minimum required is usually a professional teacher's qualification and this will suffice for the supply of most reading attainment tests and some more specialized diagnostic tests. Such tests are however sometimes made available to students for research if they are under a tutor's supervision.

Chapter One

What is a reading test?

A reading test usually consists of a test paper and a manual which contains instructions for giving, marking and interpreting the test.

The test paper will contain a number of reading tasks which can be in many forms, from single words to be read aloud to a continuous prose passage for silent reading accompanied by questions about the passage. Each task or question is known technically as an item. A pupil's reading ability is measured by his success at performing tasks or answering questions.

Standardized tests

Most published tests are standardized. This means that the test has been tried out on a large number of pupils prior to publication. The scores of this trial group provide a standard or 'norm' against which any child subsequently tested can be compared.

The group used for setting the standard should thus be typical or representative of children of their age. In this way it is possible to judge whether a particular child tested subsequently is average, below-average or above-average for his age. Age is usually a prime consideration in setting yardsticks for reading — it is after all a skill which tends to improve as the child gets older.

There are a number of ways this can be done. For example, Schonell found that the word 'saucer' was read aloud correctly from a card by half the children in a sample of eight-year-olds, but that less than half this group could read the word 'angel'. Any child who manages to read correctly from a graded word list as far as 'saucer' but no further is thus said to have reached an eight-year-old standard. In a slightly different way, it was found that about half the children of eight years could answer 14 sentence-completion questions on NFER Reading Test AD. This number was thus set as the average or normal score for children of this age.

Group tests

The most convenient tests are those which can be completed by a whole class at one sitting — group tests. These tests require a separate test-paper for each child. Group tests require that pupils work silently and write their answers on papers which are then collected and marked. The test situation is the same for everybody, and few allowances for individual differences in temperament can be made.

Individual tests

The business of learning to read usually involves the child in a fair amount of reading aloud. How well a pupil reads aloud is thus a widely used criterion of reading ability, particularly in the early stages where a child's progress through a reading scheme may depend upon how fluently he performs on his reader. If pupils are to be tested in this mode they must be tested individually — one at a time.

This is a time-consuming procedure for the class teacher to carry out. However, it is widely practised, particularly with tests which involve only re-usable materials, such as printed cards.

The test materials

A reading test can come in a number of physical parts, and for the newcomer to testing, they can constitute a confusing array of printed booklets, cards and sheets. It should therefore be helpful if we here describe what one can expect to find in a set of test materials. As with most teaching materials supplied to schools, tests can usually be obtained in inspection sets, which have to be returned to the publisher, or in specimen sets, which usually have to be purchased outright. It is highly desirable to make a close appraisal of such sample material before committing oneself to the use of a particular test.

We propose to describe firstly the most simple form a set of reading test materials can take, and then to describe the most elaborate form one might come across.

A simple set of materials

In the simplest form a group test will consist of a manual and a set of test papers — a specimen set will usually contain just one of these. The test manual will be a printed booklet with a number of sections. These will almost certainly consist of the following:

1. An introduction describing the purpose of the test, and the way in which it was developed. This should include details of the children used in the try-out work and the way the test is to be used in school.

2. A set of instructions for administering the test. This is often highly specific and detailed, specifying exactly what the teacher is to

tell the children who are to take the test, what classroom arrangements are necessary, and how much time is to be allowed. Most tests require a fairly formal and traditional kind of classroom organization, and although many primary classrooms no longer lend themselves easily to this way of doing things it is important that the administration instructions are followed as closely as possible.

3. A Marking Key. This is a list of answers to the questions and always has to be observed strictly. In most reading tests questions there is only *one* right answer, although individuals may feel from time to time that other answers could be right.

4. Conversion Tables. The number of right answers a child makes — his 'raw score' — usually doesn't mean very much on its own. In most reading tests it has to be converted to some kind of scale, such as Reading Ages, percentiles or standarized scores (see Chapter Two). This is done by looking up a raw score in a table and finding its converted or scale value. The test manual will usually include instructions on how to do this.

5. Technical Information: 1) *Reliability*. A further section in the test manual should be included which describes how 'reliable' the test is. In Chapter Two we explain what is meant by a 'reliable' test, but briefly it is one which is consistent: within the test each question should be measuring the same skill, and the test itself should be capable of giving pupils the same score if they are re-tested without having improved their reading ability in the meantime. Other bits and pieces of information may be included in the technical section, these may deal with the effects of 'guessing' on test scores, the extent to which score increases with chronological age, and any important differences in the way boys and girls perform on the test.

6. Technical Information: 2) *Validity*. The manual should also contain evidence that the test is indeed one of reading. To some extent this will be clear from an inspection of the questions themselves. They should not require specialized knowledge on the part of the reader, for example. However a test should have a little more evidence than this in its favour, such as its use in research studies on reading, agreement with other reading tests or with expert ratings of how well the children originally tested could read. The manual may also contain some discussion of what aspects of reading the test deals with, although it is usually up to the test user to decide whether the test seems to approach reading in an appropriate way. A judgement of this sort requires some knowledge about reading itself, apart from the testing of it, and this is the responsibility of the individual teacher — the test manual will not be a guide on how to teach reading. This first simple pattern also applies to some individual tests of reading, which may consist of no more than a single set of test material — perhaps just a card with words

printed on it — and a manual.

A complex set of materials

There are tests — particularly those of American origin — which are composed of a rather more elaborate set of materials. Although these are separate bits, they really only deal with the functions discussed above and the principle behind them is no different. However we will describe briefly the kind of materials one might find in a specimen set of the most elaborate sort, although in practice the majority of tests will lie somewhere between the very simple format already described and what follows.

In the first place, the test papers will involve much more than a single booklet or sheet:

1. *Equivalent forms*. Many tests are produced in more than one version, so that the teacher has the option of testing the pupil again with different test questions on a test which is in all other respects interchangeable with the one used previously.

2. *Separate answer sheets*. A test booklet or sheet which has to be written on cannot be re-used — rubbing out answers in pencil is not to be recommended! — so a system which allows the child to record his answer separately is highly desirable. This usually consists of a single sheet with numbers for the questions and some system of spaces to be shaded in or numbers to be ringed in a way which corresponds with one of a set of answer choices. These answer sheets may lend themselves to marking with a template (see below) or by computer. Some tests with separate answering systems require no more than a separate sheet of paper supplied by the test user, thus minimizing cost.

3. *Administration instructions*. An additional booklet may be printed which contains nothing more than instructions for administering the test and marking it. This has advantages of economy where a large number of people are involved in giving the test, but not necessarily in interpreting or following up the results in any way.

4. *Technical report*. This will contain an account of the construction of the test, discussion of its purpose and content, and information about reliability and validity discussed previously. Often these subjects will be written about at greater length than in a simple comprehensive manual and the report will tend to be akin to a research report in its own right.

5. *Marking keys*. A separate answer sheet may well be marked with a template, consisting of a card with holes or windows, or a perspex sheet over-printed in black. These will be designed to overlay the pupil's answer sheet or the pages of his answer book so that any right answers can be quickly identified, and wrong ones ignored. This can make

marking more rapid and less onerous. Alternatively, the correct answers may be printed on a card which has to be folded a number of times, rather like a fan, so that the correct answers can be lined up with the appropriate questions; again, this is designed to save time by guiding the marker's eye.

6. *Record forms*. A specially printed form for recording individual or group scores is sometimes provided. This will involve some form of grid or scale upon which scores can be plotted, allowing performance on different parts or sub-tests to be compared directly. The scale may be presented so that the limits or range in which a 'true' score lies can be marked — as subsequent chapters will stress, it is more accurate to regard a child's score as an *estimate* of his true standing which lies in some kind of area or corridor of error. A printed record form merely makes the marking out of this area more convenient.

Why use a reading test?

Much successful teaching of reading goes on in schools who make no use of any form of reading test. It would be foolish to claim that a child could not learn to read unless he was occasionally given a reading test. It would even be hard to show that individual children learn better in any way for being tested.

Some critics would go beyond saying that testing does no particular good, to say that it is positively harmful. There is certainly no research evidence for this and in the absence of any hard facts we should consider the main uses to which standardized tests are put by those who do feel a need for such techniques. This will not prove that such uses are beneficial, but we should remember that they reflect the needs and practices of many excellent schools and teachers.

We will then mention some of the most often quoted objections to testing — again they may be voiced by excellent reading teachers.

Information: objective vs subjective

To be effective a teacher needs a great deal of information about his pupils. In the course of day-to-day contact with his class a teacher is increasing and modifying what he knows, or thinks, about each pupil. In fact, he is continuously and informally assessing his pupils and evaluating their progress. As new information becomes available, the teacher evaluates it and sustains or modifies his approach to each child accordingly: a pupil who reads fluently on one book may be passed on to a more advanced one; another pupil who reads haltingly and inaccurately may be directed to some remedial activities or easier material. In the long run the first pupil may come to be regarded as an advanced reader, the second as backward.

In other words, the teacher is carrying out a series of very small tests each time he sets the child a task to perform or looks at what the child is doing. Much of what happens to the child is a result of this subjective 'mini-testing' by the teacher. For many purposes such informal testing is all that is required — particularly in determining what is to happen to him in the classroom from day to day or even minute to minute. In this situation though, everything depends upon the teacher's skill. One unknown quantity (the teacher) is being used to measure another — the pupil. This at least is how the situation may appear to anyone requiring information about a large number of pupils who have a number of different teachers, such as a head teacher or administrator. The standardized test is an independent source of information about how good a pupil is, which is free of any teacher idiosyncrasy and which is the same for all pupils.

Further, it is *objective* in that there is usually very little ground for debating whether a pupil has read correctly or not, or has understood the material or not. The items will have been designed for completely unambiguous marking.

Although the score on a formal test cannot hope to have the richness and sensitivity of a teacher's appraisal of a child it can claim to be free of any prejudice (however unintentional) and provide a very concise one-figure numerical summary of the much more complex information the teacher could supply given time.

It is this independence, objectivity and conciseness which make tests particularly suitable for the following practices:

1. *Ranking of pupils*. It is sometimes necessary to know which pupils in a class or larger group are better or worse than others. Their test scores may be used to put them in the required rank order.

2. *Comparison of particular children or schools with outside standards*. Much will be said later about how a representative and relevant standard or norm is established for a particular test. The point of this is to set a score which is normal or typical for the children being tested. It is this quality which makes the standardized test such a powerful instrument. The claim that a pupil (or whole school) is performing worse or better than average can be thoroughly investigated through standardized tests. By any other criterion such claims tend to remain just matters of opinion. The standard embodied in a test which has previously been tried out with children who are representative of their age groups provides a natural criterion or yardstick by which individual cases can be examined. It does not follow that any 'blame' is to be attached because a child or group falls short of the standard. However, the standard can be taken as some form of goal to be aimed for. Where there is an undue proportion of children scoring below the norm (standard) this can alert those concerned to the need for special

attention and resources.

3. *Identification of the less able*. Children who have difficulty in reading are a constant source of concern. There is a continuing need to identify these children and get an impression of the magnitude of their difficulty. The teacher will have his own first hand evidence about such a problem, but standardized testing can describe it objectively, concisely and accurately by dispassionately comparing a particular child or group with 'all children of that age'.

4. *Assessment of progress and improvement*. A pupil who is average at seven years may backslide and end up below average at nine years. It is unlikely he will have had the same teacher throughout this period and such degenerations — which are by no means uncommon — are best detected by testing. Tests also provide a convenient means of checking any improvement in the less able. Teachers will of course be in a position to notice such changes, but test information provides an authoritative verification of such insights and intuitions. The relative preciseness of a figure based on test performance may help to moderate exaggerated claims of improvement, or to encourage the despondent.

5. *Evaluation of change*. Any change in personnel, materials or methods in teaching reading is something of a step into the unknown. The trend of test results from 'before' to 'after' any change will provide objective information about its effects. This is not to suggest that tests should be the only criteria to be used; the fact remains, though, that they are one which stands beyond and outside the feelings, impressions and reports which may also be taken into consideration.

6. *Diagnosis of strengths and weaknesses*. Where a set, or battery of tests is used it is possible to detect difference and discrepancies between various reading skills. This can direct the teacher to concentrate on areas of weakness. Teachers may suspect the existence of areas of difficulty, but tests provide more precise and objective mapping-out of the problem.

Teachers vs tests?

Nothing that has been said about use of tests so far has been intended to invalidate the role of teachers in reading assessment. Nor should it be assumed that testers think teachers' judgements are hopelessly prejudiced and distorted. A subjective assessment is not necessarily a false one. Test-based assessment and teachers' judgements give different kinds of information but they are not incompatible means of assessing children. The two are best used *together*.

The justification for tests is thus that they provide certain kinds of information about children's reading ability in a form that teachers are not really in a position to supply. The argument is that we cannot teach reading effectively unless we get feedback on our efforts to confirm the worth of one approach or cast doubt on it. This process of evaluation and re-direction of teaching goes on informally in any case. But the accurate and authoritative measurement afforded by standardized tests raises this process to the level of sophistication necessary for making more important decisions about how a child is to be taught.

Criticisms of reading tests

The decision to test or not to test can only be made once a teacher becomes really clear in his own mind about the purpose and theory underlying standardized tests. In later chapters the reader will have the chance to do this. However, there are some basic misunderstandings which can be cleared up at this point:

1. *Tests are too competitive*. This is really not true of reading tests if they are used in the way intended. They are not competitive examinations; results should be confidential and no child should ever be upbraided for 'not doing well enough' on a reading test. There are no penalties or rewards attached to doing a test in the sense that there may be for weekly or termly examinations. Children who do approach a reading test with an over-competitive attitude will probably have acquired this attitude beforehand − not from the test.

2. *Some children find being tested stressful*. There are some children who get genuinely upset by the experience of being tested and who 'don't do well on tests'. Teachers should certainly have the discretionary power to withdraw such children from testing, and no test result which has been clearly distorted by nervousness should be permitted to pass without comment. These cases sometimes arouse teachers' passions, but where common sense has been exercised in initially choosing a suitable test, they are rare.

More problematic is the child who just fails to do himself justice in the test situations − perhaps because he is confused about the purpose of testing or 'allergic' to the particular mode of question used. Again, the exercise of common sense can offset any possible harm through underestimation of the child's true standing.

3. *Tests don't test what has been taught*. Unfortunately, this is too often true − there is no point in testing, say, oral word recognition if one has not been teaching word recognition skills, nor is there any sense in testing reading vocabulary if the teacher is not concerned with this skill. The fault really lies, though, with the person selecting the test. Tests should be chosen to match the stage or quality of reading which the teacher has been aiming for. It may be claimed that none of the available tests suits the teacher's purpose. This is a difficult argument to refute − however, many reading skills can be encompassed in a general test of reading vocabulary and comprehension and such tests are often

an adequate 'second best'.

4. *Teachers are there to teach, not test.* This objection is one the authors have heard many times. Class teachers certainly begrudge the time taken in test administration and marking an annual or termly set of tests. It is, however, a more potentially constructive activity than many of the other administrative chores teachers are expected to perform.

Unavoidably perhaps, children spend much time in school and class doing things other than learning. The time 'wasted' by doing tests is an insignificant portion of this. Further, teachers have to do much — even in class — which is not teaching. Lessons 'lost' through testing are again probably a miniscule quantity over the course of a term.

The need to use valuable lesson preparation time for test marking is more problematic and will only be justified if the teachers involved understand the purpose of testing in the first place and are sufficiently knowledgeable to interpret the results. Under these conditions it will be time well spent in view of the information which results.

5. *Test scores 'label' children unfairly.* Tests carry a certain authority and if misused or misunderstood can lead to children being pigeon-holed or written off. The teachers who do this on the basis of test results could probably do so even if a test had not been used; indeed, it is not uncommon for teachers to say a child has a low reading age or IQ, although no test has been given to establish this. 'John has a tested Schonell reading age of seven' we are told, 'You can't expect much of him. He'll never learn to read.' This kind of comment is sadly all too common — and quite meaningless. John's reading age has probably increased since he was tested (perhaps many months previously) and no test score on its own can tell us exactly what to expect of a child. The number of people who will 'never learn to read' is probably very small in any case. Tests are certainly not intended as a labelling device. They are an objective check on how well a child is doing at the time, to be considered alongside all kinds of other evidence about how well he is reading.

6. *You're no further on once the child has been tested.* Many schools efficiently carry out yearly testing programmes which culminate in the neat tabulation of scores in class lists. After this nothing happens; the information is not acted upon. It is all too easy either to assume that one's duty has been done once the child is tested or to feel frustrated that the test does not tell the teacher 'what to do now'. The problem behind this is often one of understanding. Test results can map out a problem, identify areas of weakness, alert teachers to undetected cases of difficulty or to confirm suspicions about particular children. For such constructive interpretations to be both made and acted upon there must be somebody around who really understands both the science of

testing and the art of teaching reading.

7. *Some tests are too complicated to be practical.* Sometimes a test will be produced which embodies many sophisticated features which are technically highly desirable but make more work for the teachers. However, the quality of information a test yields usually depends upon the amount of effort and care required to use it. The easiest and most convenient tests are probably the least useful. The same is true for many teaching materials; those that give the teacher least bother may not be the ones from which children learn best.

At the same time elaborateness should not be regarded as a virtue. If no important decisions will be influenced by the test results and a relatively simple check-up is all that is required, a more convenient test can be used. It must be admitted also that a fairly short and simple test will, if it is well constructed and carefully standardized, give similar results to more elaborate ones.

8. *Tests don't contain the kind of information teachers really want.* Teachers vary in what they want from tests and many find the tests they use give them as much information as they require about the skills they are concerned to teach.

At the same time, many experts on the psychology and teaching of reading feel the content of published tests lags behind developments in both the theory and practice of teaching reading.

In defence of reading tests it must be said that the production of new tests can really only follow developments in other areas of reading research, and few of the critics have shown how new developments can be embodied in testing methods. Nor does it follow that because a test is not quite the latest thing, it is not providing a serviceable means of measuring reading ability. It may be somewhat partial in what it measures, but it is unlikely that it is really misleading anyone. Test constructors are usually willing and anxious to be guided by the requirements and advice of teachers. However, they tend to find that when teachers are invited to write their own test materials for trials, refinement and production by technical experts, the resultant materials are really quite conventional and in no way different from existing tests.

9. *Tests only tell teachers what they already know.* In a sense the test constructors aim deliberately for this state-of-affairs. Generally they seek to devise tests which will agree with teachers' judgements. There are crucial differences in the way tests and teachers go about measuring reading performance, and this leads — perhaps in a minority of cases — to discrepancies in the way a child's reading is appraised. Tests provide a valuable second-opinion which will tend to confirm the teacher's own views but will occasionally inspire him to think again.

There are two further respects in which this criticism must be answered. In the first place, a standardized test measures a child against a national standard which lies outside the class or school. Teachers are hardly in a position to judge whether a particular child is average nationally — although he may be average for his class or school. In this the test constructor has a bird's eye view which the teacher is not placed to share. Secondly, teachers are not always in a position to get to know pupils who must, nevertheless, be tested. All children new to a class or school will come in this category, as will the child who is so anxious about his reading difficulty that he has learned to successfully conceal it from his teachers. There are indeed many circumstances where a test is required just because it *will* tend to give the same assessment a teacher would eventually come up with — given time.

10. *Test scores are spuriously precise*. Many people argue that unique human behaviour — including reading ability — cannot be reduced to mere figures. The tester's reply to this is that objective tests deal with what is common to all children and that this can be set beside the particular teacher's knowledge of what is unique to the individual child. The test task is after all, the same for all children; the performance of one child can therefore be compared with any other one or group.

Further, it must be stressed that a test score gained by a child on a particular occasion is not a fixed entity. On another occasion he might have got a few more or less items right. His score is thus only an *estimate* of his 'true' ability. Even if a child were given five identical tests on the same day it is unlikely that he would get the same score each time — though they would be similar. It follows that his standing relative to the test norm would fluctuate. The teacher could never be certain exactly how far above or below average the child was. Any one test score is thus only a pointer to where a child probably stands, within a margin of uncertainty and error. Although a test score is usually recorded as a single number, strictly speaking it is only a central point in a band of likely scores which probably cover the child's 'true' score. Accordingly, test constructors do not regard any score a child actually obtains as a precise value, free of any error or fluctuation. While most of the above criticisms have an element of justice in them, the difficulty arises as much from a misuse of standardized tests as from any inbuilt inadequacies.

Tests are by no means a flawless method of assessing children's reading. They do however have certain virtues and powers which usefully complement the subjective assessments of teachers. Many of the weaknesses of objective tests are in just those areas that the teacher's assessment can deal with so well. We have already described the unique functions filled by tests which teachers cannot fill.

It may seem lame to defend objective, standardized reading tests on the grounds that they are just misunderstood by teachers. This however happens to be the case — rare indeed is the critic who is informed about both the teaching of reading and the theory of standardized tests.

From the teacher's point of view there are two main difficulties: 1. To know what test materials are available and of their possibilities and limitations. 2. To understand the technical basis of tests and how they are to be interpreted. The following chapters deal with the latter subject, while the question of 'what is available' is tackled in subsequent chapters.

It sometimes comes as a surprise to teachers to learn that reading tests have a body of technical — mainly statistical — lore attached to them. Further, the topic is not one that is easily mastered in a single reading. Nevertheless, productive use of standardized tests really does require some understanding of the statistics involved.

The following chapters give an introduction to the subject. Ideally the reader should go on to fill-out his knowledge by reading a more specialized text. Chapters Two and Three could perhaps be left out until a second reading, but the authors would suggest that nobody should be responsible for testing children with standardized tests who was not familiar with the subjects explained in those chapters. The reader is thus urged not to completely ignore the statistical component of this book.

A note on alternatives to standardized tests

We have explained that it is the norm or standard which provides the essential reference point in objective tests. For many purposes a norm is an invaluable yardstick. However, there are a number of alternative approaches which are beginning to attract attention.

One possible method which has aroused discussion amongst test-theorists is the criterion-referenced test. In a criterion-referenced test the aim is to measure how far a child has mastered a particular skill — not how much better he is than the average. The meaning to be attached to a score is therefore one which deals with what kind of reading materials a child can master, or what kind of exercises and teaching materials would be most appropriate for him to go on to. A fuller discussion of criterion-referenced tests is included in Chapter Nine. So far few of the American tests are available in the UK and it remains to be seen how useful this kind of testing will be. The main attraction of such tests is that they claim to be measuring what children have actually learned. How valid this claim is needs much fuller examination.

A further alternative which should be mentioned is the use of checklists as a scheme of assessment. A checklist consists of a list of skills or 'things the reader can/cannot do'. As each skill or activity is mastered the teacher ticks it off. The assessment is largely subjective and relies upon the teacher's ability to make decisions as a result of informal observation. However it has the advantage of being a structured approach and provides a method of constantly checking how far the reader has progressed. Checklists have the further advantage of simplicity and freedom from technical strings. Although they lack the statistical sophistication or 'respectability' of the conventional standardized tests they are an excellent means of assessment within the classroom. They stand in fact midway between the completely informal minute-by-minute 'mini-testing' mentioned earlier, and the full-blown formality of the standardized tests given termly or less frequently. Examples of such checklists schemes are mentioned in Chapter Ten.

Chapter Two

Technical bases of reading tests

Often the content of reading tests appears to be somewhat banal. No exceptional understanding of the reading process is necessary to create a graded list of words or a series of sentences similar to those found in published tests. The distinction between a standardized test and that which a teacher might construct for his own use is primarily a statistical one. While a reading test must, of course, reflect a sound understanding of the teaching of reading, it can only be considered a reliable measuring instrument when scientific and statistical principles have been used in its construction.

Publishers of educational tests attempt to make it possible for those without special statistical knowledge to use their tests. In this they are sometimes only moderately successful, and the test user with an awareness of the underlying statistical theory of testing is in a much better position both to choose the correct test, and to interpret his results.

Teachers who attend courses on test construction and use, or on the application of statistics in education, generally are often dismayed by the technicality and abstruseness of the subject. The science of measuring behaviour or 'psychometrics' employs concepts and assumptions that are remote from everyday experience and which make great demands upon the ability to conceptualize. Many of these ideas are assimilated most easily when applied practically, and for this reason the present book contains practical suggestions and simple examples in addition to a bibliography of introductory texts. The reader could administer a short test of his own design[1] (say 10 questions) to 20 to 30 pupils so as to provide data for the examples.

The following sections deal briefly with the key statistical concepts

---

1 Chapter Four provides information likely to prove useful in devising the content of such a test.

which form part of the rationale for the construction of reading tests. Emphasis is placed upon the meaning and interpretation of the statistics and the mathematics involved is minimal.

The normal distribution

Before considering the particular statistics employed during development and use, let us turn our attention to one of the concepts fundamental to measurement in general — the notion of a distribution and, specifically, the normal distribution.

It is common experience for teachers and test constructors alike that if a test is given to a large number of candidates, a very wide range of scores will result. Some children will obtain very few marks, some will gain high marks but the majority of scores will cluster around a central value. This spreading-out or distribution of scores can be demonstrated in a block diagram showing the number of children obtaining a particular score:

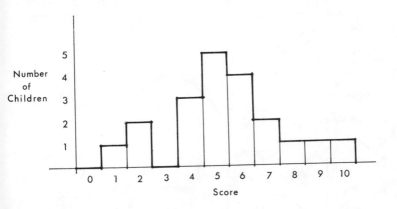

Much can be learnt about a test simply by drawing a block diagram of this type, and the reader is recommended to construct a similar score distribution for a short test of his own design. The results for a single class group of 20 to 30 would be sufficient.

For a large number of candidates taking an appropriate test we would expect to find this regular and symmetrical pattern:

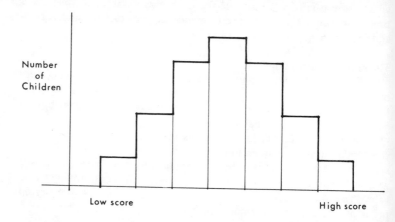

A more sophisticated way of representing this picture of the distribution of ability — and indeed many other human characteristics — involves the replacement of the separate blocks by a continuous curve:

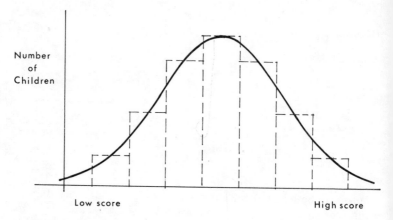

The distribution is thus seen to give the bell-shaped curve often called the curve of normal distribution.

Mean and standard deviation

The normal distribution can be completely described by two statistics; the arithmetic mean and standard deviation (SD) of the test represented by the horizontal axis. In a testing context, this is usually the test scores.

Figure 2A: The normal curve

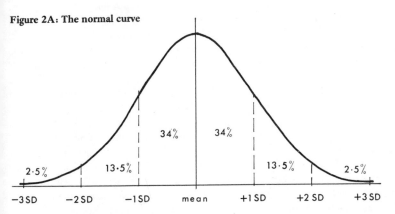

It can be seen in Figure 2A above that one standard deviation covers roughly one sixth of the mark range, and that 68 per cent of the scores fall within ±1 SD of the mean value. The use of the normal distribution as a model for test performance enables the teacher to tell, in terms of proportions, how exceptional (or otherwise) any particular score may be. It also enables him to compare with ease scores obtained on tests with different numbers of question, as all test scores can be quoted in units of standard deviation.

Some examples may help to illustrate this: in a test where the mean score is 100 and the standard deviation is 15, a score of 115 would be one SD above the mean. The pupil with this score would have a better score than 84 per cent of his peers. A score of 130 would place the pupil above 97.5 per cent of his peers. At the other extreme, a score of 85 would mean that the pupil had scored less than 84 per cent of other pupils.

It is important to note that the normal curve is only a convenient statistical 'model' for the distribution of test scores. There is no absolute reason at all why reading attainment should be normally distributed, and it is very unlikely that even the most expertly constructed test would produce a truely normal score distribution in any particular group of children. However, provided that the histogram of scores has only a single 'hump', and is fairly symmetrical about the mean value, it is an easy task to fit the data to a normal distribution with a mean and SD of whatever value is required. The scale usually applied to published tests has an arithmetic mean of 100 and a standard deviation of 15; a conversion table will be provided to convert the obtained or raw scores into standardized scores.

Sampling and standardizing

A standardized test is designed to compare pupils with their peers, and the way in which the standards of the peer group are established is clearly of critical importance. The pupils involved in standardization exercises must be representative of the population for which the test is designed. Published tests are normally intended to have the widest possible usage and so nationally representative samples are collected. However there are known to be considerable variations between local authorities, and a school which has an apparently low overall standard may in fact be superior relative to others in the area. Such internal comparisons may well be more appropriate when teachers are evaluating their efforts and test constructing organizations, such as the National Foundation for Educational Research, are often able to supply the user with information about local standards. Alternatively the local authority may have conducted its own survey — as many have in recent years — and the norms established then may be available for examination. For example, Cheshire County Education Authority has established county-wide norms for the Schonell *Graded Word Recognition Test*. (It must be pointed out though, that the local authority may wish to keep the results of its survey semi-confidential so norms are not automatically publicized or supplied to teachers.)

It is possible to assess standards nationally using a relatively small sample. However the administrative difficulties involved in obtaining such a sample are considerable and beyond the resources of most test makers. A more practical alternative is to administer the test to samples which reflect standards in more restricted areas such as local education authority areas. Under these circumstances it is often possible to test all the children of the desired age range who attend maintained schools, but it may not be easy to obtain results from directly representative areas, and often a balanced sample of authorities will have to be used: if one of the authority areas is known to be above the national norm another will have to be included which is known to be an equal amount below the national norm, so that a nationally representative picture is obtained. A published test manual will usually indicate the areas used for gathering the norms, or at least give characteristics of those areas.

Although the standardization sample is chosen to reflect the pattern of ability and standards within a particular population it can never be a perfect miniature version of the larger group. The most elaborate and sophisticated sampling methods will always contain a degree of error or uncertainty. It has been demonstrated[1] that national reading standards

---

1   See *The Trend of Reading Standards* by K.B. Start and B.K. Wells (1972) for a resume of this evidence.

are not static but have followed an upward trend since 1948 which flattened out between 1960 and 1970. It follows that the time at which the test norms were obtained will affect the accuracy with which they represent standards. The older a test is, the lower will the norms be, and, as a result, it may be over-lenient for present day pupils. It will underestimate the extent to which they are below average.

A further consideration is the time of year at which the original sample was tested. Norms for a sample of eight-year-olds obtained at the beginning of a school year, would be distinctly lower than those for the same children at the end of the school year. For example, if a teacher tests pupils at the end of the Summer term when the original sample was tested shortly after Christmas, he will be introducing an extra source of error into the results. How much error will depend upon the size of the discrepency in times of testing and the rate at which test scores increase over the year. This latter phenomenon has not been studied very fully in the past and test constructers tend to ignore it when preparing their tests.

Some published tests may have no norms at all but contain lame suggestions for schools to pool their results to develop their own norms. In such cases it is doubtful whether the purchase of the test is worthwhile in the first place. The same exercise can be carried out with tests that do have norms or indeed with teacher-made tests. Unless the publishers or constructer are definitely attempting to gather norms that will be published subsequently, such unstandardized tests should be avoided. Local norms are perhaps the bare minimum that should be provided and the preference should be to have both local and nationally-based information.

An indication of the important role which accurate sampling plays in test construction can be gained if the reader considers the choice of a standardization sample for one school. In a streamed system it would be inappropriate to test one class in an attempt to gauge the standard of the year group, whereas in a mixed-ability unstreamed system one class could represent quite an accurate sample of the year group as a whole. Similarly, the ten most able readers in any one class would not usually represent a realistic yardstick against which to measure their classmates!

Item analysis

All the items in a published test will usually have undergone a statistical analysis to ensure that they are neither too easy nor too difficult for the pupils for whom the test is intended. In addition, each item should discriminate effectively between good and weak readers if it is really measuring reading ability. The difficulty level or *facility* of an item is the proportion of candidates who respond correctly. An item with a facility of 0.50 is thus answered correctly by 50 per cent of the pupils, an item with a value of 0.35 would be correctly answered by 35 per cent of pupils.

It is useful to know the facility of each item in a test, and the reader would find it useful to investigate the proportion of children answering some of his items correctly — he will almost certainly be surprised in one or two cases! However the real importance of facility values lies in the way in which they determine how the test as a whole will behave. A mean facility of 0.50 will lead to a test which is matched to the middle range of ability and gives fairly symmetrical distribution of better and weaker readers about the average mark. Tests with lower facilities overall will spread out the better readers but leave all the weaker readers closer together. A high overall facility value will lead to the exact opposite effect. For most purposes, a test with a mean facility of 0.50 but some more difficult and some easier items is the most suitable.

The *discrimination* value of an item measures the agreement between the item and the test. If the test is accepted as an adequate measure of reading, then by comparing an item with the test as a whole it is possible to estimate the extent to which the item is an adequate test of reading. In other words, an effective item is one which is answered correctly by nearly all the better readers but by none or very few of the weaker ones.

Reliability

The reliability of a test indicates how certain we can be that a reader's score reflects his true standing and how stable an estimate it is likely to be. All test scores contain an element of error due to the uncontrollable influences which impinge upon the individual in the testing situation. If a reader completed the same test twice in one week and had no reading instruction or practice in the intervening period he would probably not get exactly the same score on both occasions.

The test constructor ensures that the size of any fluctuations is known by calculating the reliability coefficients for the test. This can be done by actually giving the test to the same pupils on two occasions and observing any differences in scores — the 'test—re-test' method. Alternatively, the internal consistency of the test may be calculated by analyzing the results of a single testing session. Where the test items are similar in form and the test is homogeneous in nature — as is the case in most reading tests — this latter approach is more appropriate. In either case an index of reliability is calculated. Perfect reliability would correspond to a value of 1.00 but in practice this is never reached. Values of .99 are exceptional and values in the range of .90 to .98 are more usual. The minimum acceptable level of reliability will depend upon the method of calculation, although as a rule internal consistency should exceed .90 while 'test-re-test' values should exceed .85.

The most common way of determing the internal consistency of a test is by splitting the test into halves and comparing the pupil's scores on the two tests thus produced. A convenient method of making this comparison is by means of a scatter diagram:

Figure 2B: Scatter diagram of odd versus even numbered items for a ten item test.

In figure 2B each single cross simultaneously represents the score of a candidate on the two halves of a ten item test. If the test in question showed perfect internal consistency (perfect reliability) then all the crosses would fall on the solid line. In the example shown in figure 2B there is considerable agreement between the two halves of the test and it can be taken as a fairly reliable instrument.

It is unlikely that most test users will ever need to calculate a reliability coefficient, but it is interesting to check by inspection of a scatter diagram that two halves of a test give similar results. The reader is recommended to try this comparison (say between odd and even numbered items) for his own test. It is unlikely however that the halves of a short test will give very similar results because each item contributes considerably to the final test score.

A more sophisticated check of internal consistency is provided by the use of the Kuder-Richardson Formula 20 (KR 20) or, more rarely, KR 21. This method takes into account the fact that a split into two halves could be obtained in a number of ways, each giving different combinations of test items. Other methods of estimating internal consistency exist, but they are rarely applied to published reading tests.

The test-re-test method has certain obvious limitations if, as one hopes, pupils are learning all the time. The attainment of the group tested is likely to progress between test sessions and since children do not all learn at the same speed, there will be changes in their relative abilities which would tend to reduce the test-re-test correlations. If the tests are given close together in time this problem is brought under control, but a direct carry over or 'training effect' may well take place, so that experience or memory of the first testing session enhances scores in the second one. An alternative is to use different versions of the same test (known as 'equivalent forms' or 'alternative forms') on each occasion. The two forms will often be made by drawing statistically similar items from a longer master-test of items to give two or more analogous tests. There will be slight differences as it is rarely possible to obtain completely identical items. This in turn weights the odds against a perfect correlation; thus equivalent-form reliability is considered to be a particularly stringent test of reliability. It is certainly very useful to have alternative versions of a test for assessing progress or carrying out long term testing policies.

Readers who wish to analyse tests of their own design for facility values, reliability, etc. will find the *Item Analysis Manual* by Nuttall and Skurnik (1970) to be of considerable help.

Chapter Three

Scales and scores

In educational testing generally a wide variety of systems for interpreting and converting raw scores to scale scores is employed. Fortunately the number of systems in use for British reading tests is relatively small. Most of the scales are interrelated, all serve to relate a pupil's performance to a norm.

Two important reservations about any system of scores must be mentioned. In the first place any test score can only lead to an *estimation* of a pupil's relative standing. If a pupil gains a score which is thought to be average for his age it is not an absolute guarantee that he *is* average. The test score is merely a single piece of evidence that he is average rather than exceptional. Nor can it be assumed with certainty that he is neither slightly above or slightly below average. A test score is thus most soundly understood as an indication of the most likely area in which a pupil's true standing lies. However his 'true' ability can never be unequivocally or absolutely determined.

The second consideration is of a more fundamental nature. Reading is a complex behaviour and to ascribe numerical values to performance on reading tasks is in a way presumptuous. In many reading situations there are no 'right' answers, while two readers may arrive at identical right or wrong conclusions by radically different means depending on the way they have been taught to read. This may apply even to the more mechanical aspects of reading — is it better to give a word-perfect but expressionless oral performance, or one which although not free of errors suggests by tone and inflection a greater sensitivity to the meaning of the text? — and it certainly applies at the higher levels of comprehension, information gathering and interpretation. The test user must be aware that in making use of any simplistic score system he is — albeit for the sake of worthwhile convenience — making considerable assumptions about the nature of reading which he should bear in mind when interpreting test results.

With these reservations in mind, some of the most common score systems can be examined.

Raw scores

A raw score is usually the number of items answered correctly, and in isolation it tells little about the quality of a pupil's performance or how much better or worse he is than other pupils. There are exceptional cases where a particular test is so well-known or important that raw scores become directly interpretable. Tests used in a large-scale survey for which the normative data are widely publicized may – for a time at least – assume direct meaning.

Raw scores may also be satisfactory where a test is being used experimentally or where strictly internal comparisons of methods or teaching materials are to be made. In general however, a test which can only supply raw scores will be of limited use.

Reading ages

The Reading Age or RA scale derives from the Mental Age system employed by intelligence tests. Early reading tests – particularly those of the single word-recognition type – were given RA values by giving items to successive age groups. When an item was passed by half the group and failed by the other half the age of that particular group was ascribed to the item as its RA value. The test would be made up of a graded series of items, each of which could be read by 50 per cent of successive age-groups. An alternative approach is to take total score distributions for an age group and assign the appropriate RA value to the mid-point or median score in the range. If half the children of eight years nine months score either side of 32 on a test the mid-point will be 32; thus a score of 32 earns an RA of eight years nine months.

A limitation of this system is that such tests give little consideration to the way scores are distributed above or below the central points. While a child who obtains an RA which exactly equals his chronological age (CA) is by definition 'average' it is hard to assess accurately the relative standing of RA scores above or below the reader's CA. In particular we may find that a year's retardation has rather different meanings (in terms of a child's position within his peer group) at different ages. The two curves of figure 3A indicate the effect which may take place between seven and 13 years of age.

At 7:0 years CA we might find that an RA of 6:0 places the pupil behind about 83 per cent of children. However a child with an RA of 12:0 at a chronological age of 13:0 may be relatively less retarded because more pupils score in the very low levels of the RA scale. There has been a progressive accumulation of children who fail to make progress in the years between seven and 13. Here a year's retardation might put a pupil behind only 70 per cent of his peers.

Figure 3A: Progressive change of reading age distribution between seven and 13 years

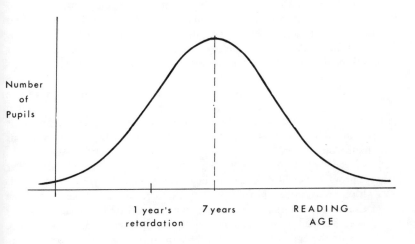

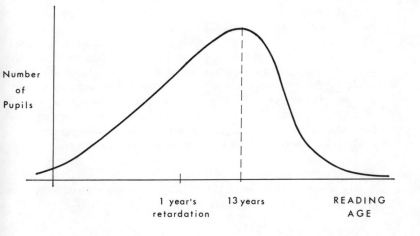

The distortion of the distribution (known as 'skewing') has an opposite effect for children who manage to gain RAs in excess of their CAs. The bunching of scores shortens the range of RAs above the median. As a result, a year's superiority of RA over CA would place a pupil above more of his peers at 13 than at seven. It follows that, as he grows older, the difference between an above average reader's RA and CA will become progressively less, without there being any change in his position relative to other children. The review of the GAPADOL Reading Test in Chapter Twelve further illustrates this point.

Thus the RA scale is more ambiguous than is generally realized, and in spite of its apparent simplicity its interpretation is not as straightforward as is sometimes assumed. There are a number of additional objections to it and these are listed briefly below:

1. Reading does not develop in a linear or exact relationship to age; to interpret scores as if they bore an exact correspondence to age when age and score are *not* perfectly correlated is misleading. Development of reading ability follows a series of slopes and plateaux, not a continuous single slope.

2. To determine a reading age scale, we may either take particular age groups of children and find their average *score*, or take all the pupils with a given score and find their average *age*. For example, to take an extreme case, suppose that every nine-year-old taking a particular test scores 31, and so do an equal number of 10:0-year-olds. The average score of the age group 9:0 is 31, but the average age of the score group 31 is 9:6. A score of 31 can mean either a reading age of 9:0 or 9:6, again the RA concept is ambiguous.

3. Tests in other areas of ability and attainment rarely use age-scales; in view of the desirability of comparing reading test scores with other educational attainments RAs tend to be inconvenient.

4. No test score is either exact or permanent, yet all too often it is said that a child 'has' a particular RA long after the time of testing. The obtained RA score is only an estimate of the child's attainment and it is likely that his 'true' RA lies somewhat above or below test score. An RA will in any case only apply at the time of testing and there will be a tendency for it to increase later; it is not a fixed property of a reader.

Any test score can only be an approximate value which has a degree of error and uncertainty associated with it. More sophisticated scales have some standard method of indicating what the margin of error is likely to be, but often the RA scale does not lend itself to this.

Reading quotients

The discrepancy between RA and CA can be represented directly by forming a 'quotient' using the formula:

$$\text{Reading Quotient} = \frac{\text{Reading Age}}{\text{Chronological Age}} \text{ x } 100$$

The 'average' reader will earn a Reading Quotient (RQ) of 100. Where RA exceeds CA the resulting quotient will be more than 100 and where RA is less than CA the RQ will be less than 100.

This approach directly states 'retardation' and 'advancement' but an error due to skewing of the score distribution (Figure 3A) will be compounded. Reading quotients suffer from the same lack of uniformity of meaning at varying ages as do RAs. Incidentally the concept of IQ — based on considerations of Mental Age and Chronological Age — involves very similar difficulties.

It must be noted that many published tests give tables for converting raw scores into quotients which are in fact deviation quotients and synonymous with the standardized scores discussed later. Test users should read the manual accompanying the test very carefully to determine whether the scores are genuine quotients or in fact standardized scores. Almost invariably the latter is really being used.

Percentiles

Some reading tests state scores as percentiles or percentile equivalents. A score above the 32nd percentile would exceed the scores of only 32 per cent of the population. A score below the 52nd percentile would be exceeded by the scores of 52 per cent of the population. Percentiles represent points which divide populations into two portions. For this reason a score is usually interpreted as being above or below a percentile, not *at* any particular percentile. However a percentile *equivalent* may be interpreted as showing a score is above or *equal to* the stated percentage.

Deciles

Occasionally a simpler grading than percentiles is required in which percentiles are grouped into ten equal units or 'deciles'. The seventh decile thus corresponds to the 70th percentile, the eighth decile to the 80th percentile and so on.

Standardized scores

The scale most widely used by modern reading tests is the standardized score system. Such scores are sometimes erroneously referred to as quotients because of the use of 100 to designate the average score. Standardized scores however do not involve chronological age but take the raw score mean for a sample and give this the value of 100. The standard deviation is arbitrarily set at 15 so that the majority of scores — 68 per cent — should fall in the range of 85 to

115, and the standardized scores will correspond with the proportions indicated by the standard deviation.

Figure 3B: Standardized Score distribution.

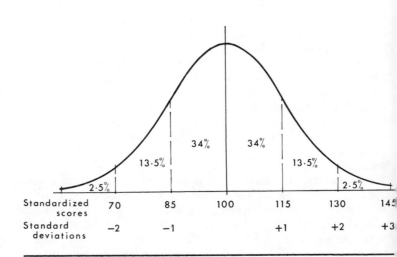

Even if the underlying distribution is skewed there will still be a direct correspondence between standardized scores and percentiles as indicated in Table 3A as the converted scores are made to fit the normal curve pattern. Tests employing the standardized score system often provide separate tables for each age group on a month by month basis. This is because the increase of score with age makes it necessary to provide some form of age-adjustment so that children of different ages can be compared fairly. A high score at 8:0 may well appear to be mediocre at 9:0. A pupil may seem to be a poor reader only because he is being compared with older children. When compared with his own age group, calculated to the nearest month, he may emerge as an average reader or better.

Figure 3C contains a typical example of a conversion table, which enables the raw scores of children between 6:10 and 8:0 who have attempted the vocabulary sections of the *Gates MacGinitie Primary A Reading Tests* to be converted to raw scores.

The raw score values are presented in the extreme left-hand and

Table 3A: The relationship between standardized scores and percentiles

Standard-ized Score	Per-centile	Standard-ized Score	Per-centile	Standard-ized Score	Per-centile	Standard-ized Score	Per-centile	Standard-ized Score	Per-centile
		130	97.9	115	84.9	100	51.3	85	16.7
		129	97.5	114	83.3	99	48.7	84	15.1
		128	97.1	113	81.6	98	46.0	83	13.6
		127	96.7	112	79.7	97	43.4	82	12.2
		126	96.1	111	77.8	96	40.8	81	10.9
140	99.7	125	95.5	110	75.0	95	38.2	80	9.7
139	99.6	124	94.9	109	73.7	94	35.7	79	8.6
138	99.5	123	94.1	108	71.5	93	33.3	78	7.6
137	99.4	122	93.3	107	69.1	92	30.9	77	6.7
136	99.3	121	92.4	106	66.7	91	28.5	76	5.9
135	99.1	120	91.4	105	64.3	90	26.3	75	5.1
134	98.9	119	90.3	104	61.8	89	24.2	74	4.5
133	98.7	118	89.1	103	59.2	88	22.2	73	3.9
132	98.5	117	87.8	102	56.6	87	20.3	72	3.3
131	98.2	116	86.4	101	54.0	86	18.4	71	2.9
								70	2.5

right-hand columns and the corresponding standardized scores are tabulated in successive columns for each age group.

The tables are used by cross-plotting a child's raw score with his chronological age. For example, if Johnny aged 7:4 scores 21 on the test, he gets a standardized score of 90. Similarly a child of 6:10 with a raw score of 30 earns a standardized score of 100 — average for his age. If an 8:0-year-old earned such a raw score he would be classified as distinctly less than average for his age, with a converted score of only 88.

The use of separate tables for each age group is most important when the rate of increase of score with age is steep. This is most prevalent during critical periods of learning such as that during and subsequent to initial reading teaching. In such a period a raw score value will decrease steeply in standardized score value from month to month because attainment is affected by the age of the child. Amongst older readers slope in the rate of increase will become progressively less, until between about 15 and 18 it slackens off completely.

Extrapolated scores

A table of standardized scores will indicate a general trend and rate of increase of attainment with age. If a test user is prepared to assume that this increase would continue in a linear and unabated way for children outside the age range actually tested, the tables can be extended to cover older and younger children. If a raw score of 30 is worth 100 points at eight years and 95 at nine years it would follow that it would be expected to be worth 90 at ten years, allowing for an adjustment of five points of standardized score over 12 months. Similarly it might be expected to be worth 105 at seven years.

Some test constructors will state a value for extrapolation which they consider reasonable. This value, sometimes called an 'extrapolation coefficient' can be used to extend the tables to cover ages not actually tested. To do this the standardized score for any raw score is found for a child exactly 12 months younger or older. The coefficient is then added if the child actually tested is younger, or subtracted if he is older.

Test constructors are reluctant to publish extrapolation coefficients as they are based on the assumption of a linear progression. In fact the development is usually *curvilinear* so an extrapolated score will overestimate scores for older children and underestimate them for younger children. In any case some part of the published tables may already be extrapolated. However, the teacher may need to use the technique where a few children in a group are not covered by the published tables and there is justification for a 'scientific guess'.

Figure 3C: Conversion Tables (Raw Score to Standardized Score) for *The Gates MacGinitie Primary A Reading Test Vocabulary*

Test Raw Score	6.10	6.11	7.00	7.01	7.02	7.03	7.04	7.05	7.06	7.07	7.08	7.09	7.10	7.11	8.00	Test Raw Score
0																0
1																1
2	71	70														2
3	74	73	72	71	70											3
4	76	75	74	73	72	72	71	70								4
5	78	77	76	75	74	73	72	72	71	70						5
6	79	78	78	77	76	75	74	73	72	72	71	70				6
7	81	80	79	78	77	76	76	75	74	73	72	71	71	70		7
8	82	81	80	80	79	78	77	76	75	75	74	73	72	71	70	8
9	83	83	82	81	80	79	78	78	77	76	75	74	73	73	72	9
10	85	84	83	82	81	81	80	79	78	77	76	76	75	74	73	10
11	86	85	84	83	83	82	81	80	79	78	78	77	76	75	74	11
12	87	86	85	85	84	83	82	81	80	80	79	78	77	76	75	12
13	88	87	87	86	85	84	83	82	81	81	80	79	78	77	76	13
14	89	88	88	87	86	85	84	83	82	82	81	80	79	78	77	14
15	90	89	88	88	87	86	85	84	83	83	82	81	80	79	78	15
16	91	90	89	88	88	87	86	85	84	83	83	82	81	80	79	16
17	92	91	90	89	88	88	87	86	85	84	83	83	82	81	80	17
18	93	92	91	90	89	88	88	87	86	85	84	83	82	82	81	18
19	93	92	92	91	90	89	88	87	87	86	85	84	83	82	82	19
20	94	93	92	91	90	89	89	88	87	86	86	85	84	83	83	20
21	95	94	93	92	91	90	90	89	88	87	86	85	85	84	83	21
22	95	94	94	93	92	91	90	89	88	88	87	86	85	84	83	22
23	96	95	94	93	92	92	91	90	89	88	87	87	86	85	84	23
24	96	96	95	94	93	92	91	91	90	89	88	87	86	85	85	24
25	97	96	95	94	94	93	92	91	90	89	89	88	87	86	85	25
26	98	97	96	95	94	93	92	92	91	90	89	88	87	87	86	26
27	98	97	96	96	95	94	93	92	91	90	90	89	88	87	86	27
28	99	98	97	96	95	94	94	93	92	91	90	89	88	88	87	28
29	99	98	97	97	96	95	94	93	92	91	91	90	89	88	87	29
30	100	99	98	97	96	95	95	94	93	92	91	90	90	89	88	30
31	100	99	98	98	97	96	95	94	93	93	92	91	90	89	88	31
32	101	100	99	98	97	96	96	95	94	93	92	91	91	90	89	32
33	101	100	99	99	98	97	96	95	94	94	93	93	91	90	89	33
34	102	101	100	99	98	97	97	96	95	94	93	92	92	91	90	34
35	102	101	100	100	99	98	97	96	95	95	94	93	92	91	90	35
36	103	102	101	100	99	98	98	97	96	95	94	93	93	92	91	36
37	103	102	102	101	100	99	98	97	97	96	95	94	93	92	91	37
38	104	103	102	101	100	100	99	98	97	96	95	95	94	93	92	38
39	104	104	103	102	101	100	99	99	98	97	96	95	94	93	93	39
40	105	104	104	103	102	101	100	99	99	98	97	96	95	94	94	40
41	106	105	105	104	103	102	101	100	100	99	98	97	96	95	95	41
42	107	107	106	105	104	103	102	102	101	100	99	98	97	97	96	42
43	109	108	107	107	106	105	104	103	102	101	101	100	99	98	97	43
44	111	110	109	109	108	107	106	105	104	104	103	102	101	100	99	44
45	114	113	112	111	110	110	109	108	107	106	105	104	104	103	102	45
46	117	116	115	115	114	113	112	111	110	110	109	108	107	106	105	46
47	122	121	120	119	119	118	117	116	115	114	113	113	112	111	110	47
48	131	130	129	128	127	126	126	125	124	123	122	121	121	120	119	48

T-scores

A few tests employ a scale known as T-scores. These are similar to the standardized scores in that they reflect units of standard deviation. The mean of the scale is set at 50 and the standard deviation at 10. This system is rarely used in British reading tests.

Standard error

From a knowledge of the reliability of a test it is possible to estimate the error which accompanies its administration. The statistical details of the procedure are not important here, but the standard error often quoted for published tests refers to the distribution of errors in the same way as a standard deviation refers to the distribution of scores. We can thus see that 68 per cent of measured scores will fall within ±1 SE either side of the 'true' score and that 95 per cent will fall within ±2 SE either side of the 'true' score.

Figure 3D: Distribution of errors of measured scores, either side of the 'true' score.

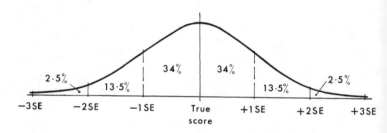

It is a useful rule of thumb, when considering the scores of two pupils from the same test (or of one pupil from two different tests) that only differences greater than twice the standard error should be considered significant. For example, if a test has a standard error of three, and a pupil obtains a score of 102 a second pupil must score at least more than 108 (or at most, less than 96) before we can conclude that there is a genuine difference in their respective attainment. When comparing scores from two tests with different standard errors, a discrepancy of twice the *larger* of the two errors is the smallest difference which can be considered genuine.

A test for which no reliability value or standard error is reported should be treated with suspicion, particularly if it is relatively short. As has been mentioned above, short tests tend to give less satisfactory reliability values and hence larger standard errors. Continuous prose comprehension tests should also be examined with care as they tend to be statistically slightly less reliable than simpler and more mechanical tests.

When a test is spoken of as being standardized, this usually means that satisfactory norms have been established. However the technical procedures of item analysis and reliability study should have been carried out as a matter of course prior to any publication for general use. Indeed it is often the practice to carry out checks on reliability and item statistics both before and after full standardization.

Guessing

Some test manuals report work done on the influence of guessing on scores during test construction. In the case of multiple-choice items teachers may wonder to what extent guessing or random answering has inflated the scores of the less able readers. They may feel that the conclusion reached by the constructor, usually that guessing does not influence scores, is at odds with their own observations.

The authors suspect that both test constructors and teachers are right, but are looking at the problem from different viewpoints. It is probably the case that guessing or wild selection of answers in desperation makes little difference to the overall technical soundness of the test. However the teacher is much more likely to be struck by the anomalies arising where one or two children who are known to be very poor readers gain spuriously high marks through chance.

The test user should follow the rule that any raw score which equals or is less than that which could be gained by chance alone should be ignored. Thus on a 30 item test in which five alternatives are supplied for each item, scores equal to or lower than six should be discarded or treated with the utmost suspicion.

This procedure needs to be qualified however: where a pupil answers the first few items correctly, then fails to give any response to any subsequent items it is likely that he has refused to guess, and exercised a form of self-regulation. Such a case is very different from that in which a pupil answers every item in the test but gets roughly only one in five — or whatever the likely guessing rate is — correct, with few consistent correct answer sequences. Here the probability that the pupil has been 'playing the odds' is higher.

A further consideration should be that in selecting the test in the first place the teacher should ensure that it would be unlikely that the reader in need of remedial help could escape detection or identification, even if he did guess. It should be possible by inspecting the norms provided to ensure that the guessing score is still way below average. This is important as a number of published tests render average scores that are uncomfortably close to guessing scores. Such a case is particularly likely to occur where tests are intended for a very wide age range.

Interpretation of test scores

The reader may by now feel that considerable statistical knowledge is necessary to successfully interpret test results. This is not the case; in fact a great deal of information can be extracted from test scores without the use of any statistical technique other than counting! To illustrate this point, the reader is invited to work through the following short exercise. The later questions give an indication of useful strategies to adopt, but no answers are given since none exist. The interpretation of statistics is not an exact science but essentially a matter of individual judgement.

Question 1

Here are the standardized scores for a group of seven-year-olds who have taken tests of Reading and Non-Verbal Reasoning. (The standardized score system is briefly explained on pages 39–42).

Pupil	Non-Verbal Reasoning	Reading	Pupil	Non-Verbal Reasoning	Reading
01	100	96	21	87	74
02	106	101	22	101	94
03	87	77	23	101	99
04	75	70	24	107	106
05	111	106	25	107	100
06	96	90	26	77	70
07	125	121	27	94	85
08	70	70	28	116	104
09	135	137	29	104	99
10	100	94	30	82	70
11	94	90	31	131	123
12	105	100	32	104	99
13	128	113	33	82	70
14	86	83	34	117	113
15	102	93	35	110	102
16	97	91	36	120	144
17	96	87	37	86	77
18	89	84	38	95	86
19	113	106	39	84	100
20	116	111	40	110	105

Pupil	Non-Verbal Reasoning	Reading	Pupil	Non-Verbal Reasoning	Reading
41	79	72	66	102	96
42	109	98	67	82	75
43	90	81	68	91	81
44	95	92	69	111	100
45	120	120	70	99	92
46	71	71	71	122	122
47	85	78	72	124	116
48	140	129	73	124	119
49	95	90	74	105	101
50	95	81	75	87	78
51	108	99	76	83	75
52	80	72	77	103	96
53	92	85	78	96	92
54	114	118	79	107	102
55	89	110	80	94	84
56	105	95	81	101	91
57	109	95	82	129	116
58	92	79	83	113	99
59	99	92	84	101	101
60	118	100	85	110	108
61	104	94	86	119	116
62	90	83	87	74	70
63	98	91	88	141	130
64	99	90	89	114	102
65	106	94	90	99	91

a) Do the figures suggest that the group is generally of average, above average or below average standard?

b) Which pupils would you select for special help in Reading?

Question 2
Standards

In a completely average and representative sample of children the *proportion* of children scoring in the major score bands (Standard Deviations) would be as follows.

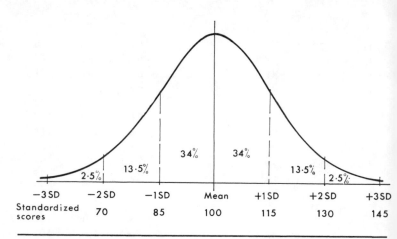

Now check the distribution of scores for one or both of the tests for which you have results in Question 1.

Does this confirm the conclusion already reached?

Question 3
Backwardness
   Technically, any child with a standardized score less than 100 is 'backward for his age'. Children with scores below 100 but above about 90 are still 'fairly average'. A score of less than 90 places a child in the bottom 25 per cent of his age group.

Check Table 3A on page 41 to determine roughly what percentrage of
   pupils would be classified as backward by your standard.

Question 4
Backwardness and Ability
a) The results of Non-Verbal tests are sometimes used to identify poor readers who are nevertheless mentally bright. Are there any such pupils in the group under consideration? (the standard error of the Non-Verbal test is four and of the Reading test is three).
b) Non-Verbal tests are also sometimes taken as a general indicator of mental ability. If this is justified, what do the results say about the

relationship between ability and attainment in the present results? (see Question 2).

Discussion

1a) It is not necessary to determine the exact mean scores on either test for the group as a whole, although this is always instructive at the class level. Question Two gives a sufficiently accurate method for determining how average a group is. For a quick guide, we can see that 41 pupils scored less than 100 on the non-verbal test and 56 pupils scored less than 100 on the reading test. We can provisionally conclude that the group is slightly above average in non-verbal ability but below average in reading.[1]

1b) This is a matter of personal judgement, but see Question Three.

2. The distributions are as follows:

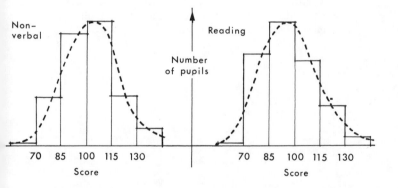

These confirm the provisional conclusions reached in 1a).

3. Local factors such as the availability of resources always weigh very heavily in deciding how many pupils should be given remedial help. However a score of less than 85 means that the child's attainment is lower than 84 per cent of his peers and is always cause for concern. There are 24 such pupils in the group shown.

4a. As a rule of thumb, any child whose scores on the two tests have a

---

1 See page 75 for discussion of the relationship between the Non-Verbal test performance and reading ability.

discrepancy of more than *twice the larger standard error* may be suspected of underachieving. Since the standard error of the non-verbal test is four, a difference of eight or more is significant; there are 36 such pupils in the group shown.

4b. It is clear that the reading scores are generally lower than the non-verbal scores. The mean score on the non-verbal test is 101.8 and on the reading test is 95.2. There are three possible explanations for this:

a. The reading test is giving pessimistic results (either standardization or content may be out of date, or inappropriate to these children).

b. The non-verbal test may be giving optimistic results (again standardization may be at fault, or these children may have received practice in this sort of test).

c. Provided 1 and 2 are not the case (it is often advisable to check these points with the test publishers since they will usually have records of the behaviour of the tests), we can conclude that there is a genuine difference between non-verbal ability and reading attainment in the group concerned.

Chapter Four

The content of reading tests

One of the greatest pitfalls in testing reading is the use of a test which is inappropriate in content for the child being tested. In particular there is a danger that tests will be chosen exclusively because of their simplicity in content and administration. As a result the reader's performance gets to be evaluated on the basis of tasks which are unrelated to those he will subsequently be expected to do or has recently learned to do.

Graded Word Recognition Tests (GWRTs) such as those of Burt, Vernon and Schonell are particularly prone to this danger. These involve reading unrelated and individual words from a list. However, unless a pupil has been taught in this way, or will be expected to perform this task in class (surely highly unlikely!) the use of these lists as a guide to what has been learned will be limited except as a very rough and general yardstick.

Convenience vs. relevance

There are many simplistic tests available which appeal because of their convenience to administer and low cost. However, the aim of this book is to suggest ways in which assessment might be improved in schools, and one improvement that is particularly desirable would be greater concern for a match between the criteria of assessment and the nature of what is being taught: the content of the test must be tailored to the learner just as much as teaching techniques and learning materials should be. In principle we should only restrict testing to those things which are 'convenient to test' if we are prepared to restrict teaching to things which are 'convenient' to teach.

How strictly such a principle should apply depends on the purpose of testing. However there are clearly many situations in which there is too little relationship between the reading test and the reading curriculum. For example, many junior schools administer a final test before their pupils leave to enter secondary schools. The most common test for this purpose is a GWRT, yet such a test refers mainly to skills acquired much earlier in school life, and hardly does justice to the scope of much top junior work. In particular it neglects all kinds of more advanced skills which should have been developed in the later junior years.

'All reading tests measure the same thing'

Every so often a research study will be published which will show that a number of reading tests are all highly 'correlated'. This means that statistically they agree about who the good readers are, and who the less able are. They may also tend to give the same reading 'age' or standardized score to a particular child, although they tend to be less consistent in this respect because their standardizations may be from different times and different samples of children.

It is notable that GWRTs give similar results to more elaborate and seemingly searching rests. A teacher might therefore wonder why it is necessary to become involved with a less convenient kind of test if it is not going to give him a substantially different result.

To answer this, a number of related points must be considered.

Because two tests correlate statistically, it does not follow that they are measuring the same thing. For example, verbal reasoning tests tend to correlate highly with most tests of educational attainment. However we would not necessarily substitute a verbal reasoning test for a test of mathematics or geography, and we would certainly not give up teaching mathematics in favour of verbal reasoning lessons!

Two abilities may be so closely associated as to be. statistically interchangeable, but they are not necessarily educationally interchangeable. The content of the curriculum is selected on the basis of what is important and worthwhile and if assessment is to become a legitimate part of the curriculum the same rule should apply.

The simple skills such as word recognition form a foundation for the acquisition of more advanced skills. The child who does well in learning the early skills will do better in acquiring the later ones. However these skills still have to be learned and there will still be individual variations in the extent to which children acquire them. For example, in an hypothetical group of children who all have the same word recognition skill the scores on a test of more advanced skills would still probably vary. Most would probably do well, but some could be expected to do better than others, a few might even do rather poorly, showing they had not really mastered the subsequent skills.

Strictly speaking, it is the means of tests which are correlated, rather than individual scores. Even when correlations are high, these will be individual cases where there are educationally significant differences. These will only occur in a minority of cases, but from the teacher's point of view these could well prove to be the most important ones, for example, the child who can read aloud fluently, without the least idea of the meaning of what he is reading.

Some skills probably correlate in research findings simply because the researchers have chosen to test in areas where no teaching goes on. For example, the *Edinburgh Reading Tests* employ two sub-tests dealing with: 1) Retention of Main Ideas and 2) Comprehension of Point of View, yet one doubts that serious conscious efforts are often made to teach these two skills and there is no reason why a child left to his own devices to develop these skills should become more proficient in one than the other. Accordingly, it is hardly surprising they appear to be correlated. If, for some reason a teacher actively taught one skill but not the other, the relationship between them would possibly be diminished.

Testing reading without teaching it

We have discussed the problem of employing a test which does not really fit the children or the type of teaching involved. The danger of using reading tests in the absence of any teaching at all should be mentioned. Strictly speaking, there is no point in going to the trouble and expense of giving attainment tests in a subject area which is not actually being taught. Some reading specialists would certainly regard the skill as one which should be actively taught throughout the junior and secondary years. 'If it is not being taught', they could argue 'then why bother to test it?'

In practice schools do feel a need to check up on reading progress even though much of the learning is incidental and informal rather than as a result of direct teaching, so that special teaching can be given if found necessary. Throughout the middle years the reading ability of the average child does increase — reading is a skill he has to use and develop every day in a wide range of contexts. It is important to make sure that progress is being made but the reader of this book might pause to ask himself whether part of the concern about testing national standards of reading at say, 11 years and 15 years might be directed towards a policy of teaching more fully at these ages. Testing is no substitute for teaching.

The development of reading ability

There is not space to fully describe what happens when a pupil reads. Like much human behaviour it is extremely complex, and researchers have yet to produce a conclusive and comprehensive description of what happens when a child reads. Clay (1972a) and Gaspar and Brown (1973) provide examples of recent works on this topic. However it would be as well to mention some of the skills which are acquired at each of the main stages in learning to read, so that

ensuing discussion of reading test-tasks can be related to them:

1. *Pre-Reading Skills.* The idea of 'reading readiness' is often regarded with suspicion because of the mistaken teaching practices which sometimes arise from it, such as elaborate forms of perceptual training which seem to have no carry-over into learning to read. However, development of pre-reading skills is a legitimate part of teaching reading and certain aspects of physical and psychological development do have to be considered in giving appropriate teaching. These range from considerations of health, nutrition, sight, vision and emotional well-being to those of perceptual, linguistic and mental development.

2. *Word-Recognition Skills.* Most approaches to the early teaching of reading take the *word* as the basic unit of teaching, even though the teaching may emphasize the learning of words in context from the very beginning. Thus the skills and processes involved in reading words are a first consideration in the development of reading ability.

3. *Intermediate Reading Skills.* Reading is not simply a matter of being able to recognize the sound and meaning of individual and isolated words, nor when the reader recognizes individual words is he using only information or cues *within* the word itself. In addition to phonic knowledge and sound blending skills the pupil will make increasing use of his knowledge of the probabilities and structural rules which give pattern to language and the context which surrounds the word.

At the same time, as the child acquires reading skill, he will be expected to make use of this skill in increasingly demanding situations. He will, as a minimum, have to understand, remember and make use of simple and explicit information presented in continuous sentence form. In turn this skill will make mechanical word recognition an increasingly redundant skill.

4. *Extended Comprehension Skills.* In the middle years of education the child will have to make increasing use of continuous prose reading skills. They are the means by which independent work becomes possible. Furthermore, these will have to be used with increasing sophistication. To the intermediate comprehension skills will be added more inferential and judgmental reading. There will be a greater emphasis on flexibility of reading and capacity to read for different purposes. Ultimately, these may develop into the advanced study skills necessary for academic work in secondary school.

Oral vs. silent reading

As reading ability is developed through these main stages there is a decreasing emphasis upon knowing the sounds of the written words —

oral reading. The requirements of the classroom will increasingly stress 'reading for meaning' so reading becomes more and more a private, silent activity. If the child fails to develop skills in this activity he will not be able to use reading for one of its most important and rewarding purposes: to enter the world of the author and enjoy the extension of his world and experience through the printed word. It is only in remedial teaching that the older pupil will be involved substantially in reading aloud.

This change of emphasis accords with recent theories about the nature of reading. These tend to speak of a radical difference between the way a beginner and a fluent reader operate. Goodman (1968) for example describes three stages in reading. In the first the learner proceeds from printed words to the sounds they make, before decoding these as language and then meaning. He suggests an intermediate stage in which the reader proceeds directly to language and thence to meaning, and a final stage of fluency in which printed information is perceived directly in terms of its meaning. It follows that although many reading tests may be concerned with the pupil's knowledge of the sound values of print — grapheme (print) /phoneme (sound) correspondence — this may be misplaced as a method of assessing readers who have progressed beyond the initial decoding skills.

Bearing in mind the implications of qualitative changes with age in the strategies which the reader employs and the demands made upon him in school as a reader, together with the relative values of oral and silent reading as means of assessment at various stages, we will now consider the various techniques employed in published reading tests:

Word recognition

For a long time the ability to read through a list of progressively 'harder' words was taken as the criterion of reading attainment, and the Burt, Vernon and Schonell GWRTs are still the most frequently used reading tests.

Simple word-recognition is however an inadequate model of reading, particularly once the initial decoding skills have been acquired. Moreover these tests tend to have rather dated norms and the order of word-difficulty has probably changed since the original sequence was devised due to changes in vocabulary over the years. A more meaningful measure of the young reader's ability to orally decode common words could probably be obtained using a sample of words from a word-count list such as that found in McNally and Murray (1964). This is a list of the 200 most common printed words, and the authors claim it accounts for up to 70 per cent of children's reading and a substantial proportion of adult reading. The words are presented as a test list as well as a teaching list; the test is, however, rarely used. This is a pity as it would have considerable use as a 'criterion-referenced' test. This could be done quite easily by taking a random sample of, say, 30 words and having the pupil read them. The result would indicate the extent to which the pupil could deal competently with a substantial amount of the reading material he will meet. Most of the common structural words of English are included in this list, so the result might also give an indication of particular difficulty with this aspect of language. For teaching purposes this is surely a more useful mode of assessment than a standardized word recognition test. There is, after all, very little point in actually teaching Schonell's or Burt's words as they were selected on entirely statistical grounds. If McNally and Murray's 'Keywords' were used there would be a positive virtue in 'teaching to the test'.

Sophisticated alternatives for assessment at the word-recognition level can be found in group tests such as the Carver's *Word Recognition Test*. Here a group testing situation is used to obtain a 'Word Recognition Age'. This corresponds not to a gross increase in the number of words recognized but to a sequence in the development of phonic skills. This test differs from traditional tests of word recognition in holding that Word Recognition Age ceases to be a meaningful concept above about 8:06 years. The Carver Test requires the pupil to find the printed word to go with its spoken version — as opposed to producing spoken forms to match their printed equivalents. The test paper contains a series of items like the following:

LGO	LOG	YOG	GOL	LIG	HUG
MOOD	MADE	MAD	MOFE	MIDE	

The test manual contains a master list of target words to be read out by the teacher, for example 'log' and 'made', and the child has to identify these from the set printed on the test page.

A similar technique is used by the *Swansea Test of Phonic Skills*. Here a non-meaningful spoken word is given and its printed phonic representation has to be identified on the test paper.

WIK	NURT	NAUG	
TIK	NURN	NIOG	
RIK	NUST	NEIG	(not from
KIK	NUFT	NEEG	original test)
SIK	NUCK	NOOG	

Again some indication of phonic progress in qualitative form is possible with this test.

Neither the GWRTs, Swansea nor the Carver Tests examine the pupil's knowledge of the correspondence between words and their referents, i.e. their meaning. This is possible with the vocabulary section of the *Gates-McGinitie Reading Tests* (Primary A: Vocabulary), where printed words have to be matched with the appropriate pictures. A more fundamental test of a child's knowledge of word meanings is provided by the *English Picture Vocabulary Tests* in which a picture has to be matched with a word spoken by the tester — no reading in involved. This is sometimes regarded as a test of mental ability, but it would also indicate in crude terms how far the teaching of word-recognition skill would in fact be meaningful to the learner. A child who cannot associate spoken words with objects will hardly find it easy to associate printed words with objects and will certainly be ill-equipped to make use of meaning in his reading.

Simple word recognition skills can thus be tested in very different ways, with varying emphases upon mechanics or meaning. The optimal form of testing at this level would combine a test of meaning with one of phonics. There is however some case for thinking that a picture/word matching test gets closest to combining the two functions in one test: the child sees the picture, recognizes its sound value in his head or by sub-vocalizing, then chooses the printed word which matches this sub-vocalized sound impression. The *Gates-McGinitie Test*, and to a lesser extent the *Southgate Group Reading Test 1* would meet this requirement, but neither test provides such a systematic guide to the development of phonics in itself as the Carver test.

Sentence reading

Testing capacity to orally read whole sentences is perhaps slightly more satisfactory, as the reader's intonation and stress may provide fuller indications of the degree of comprehension, while his capacity to tackle unfamiliar words via information outside the individual word itself is brought into play. Traditional phonic methods teach the reader to concentrate upon information or 'cues' which are contained *within* the word in question. However fluent reading is greatly assisted if the reader can use information outside the word such as the need for syntactical agreement and intonation. These aid him to avoid or correct such misreadings as '. . . than I fell' for '. . . then I fell' (syntax) or 'the boys runs' for 'the boy runs' (intonation). In addition, the actual meaning of other words in the sentence provides a valuable aid to 'zeroing-in' on the correct reading of a phonically difficult or unfamiliar word. Again, efficient use of such 'guesswork' is an important characteristic of the fluent reader.

The sentence is thus perhaps the minimum acceptable level of assessment for any purpose beyond the teaching of initial word decoding skills. At the same time, it cannot be assumed that a mechanical test of sentence reading will give the same result as a more searching sentence-based silent comprehension test. One suspects that reliance on the results of oral sentence-reading tests leads to increasingly misleading conclusions as pupils grow older. A pupil whose reading appears to be satisfactory by the standard of an oral sentence-reading test given in junior school may still not have developed the wider ranging reading skills adequate to the demands of secondary school work.

The oral sentence test will always have application with backward or disabled readers, but it may lead to hopelessly optimistic assumptions about real-life capabilities of many supposedly 'average' readers. The *Holborn Reading Scale* and Sub-test 1 of Daniels and Diack's *Standard Reading Tests* are the two most widely used sentence reading tests, but their norms are probably somewhat dated.

Continuous prose reading

Sustained oral reading of passages is a task which approximates to some real-life classroom demands. Its use recently has been largely confined to one test, the *Neale Analysis of Reading Ability* which has a primarily diagnostic function, although attainment scores are obtained for mechanical fluency, rate and comprehension. Continuous prose tests such as this allow full play for the reader's use of contextual cues beyond those contained within the word or sentence to be used. In effect they provide the best context for testing intelligent mechanical reading. A teacher can assess prose reading ability using reading material of his own choice in the form of the *Informal Reading Inventory* (IRI). This technique does not allow any normative score to be obtained, but is useful as a diagnostic technique, or as a means of assessing how well a child is likely to cope with a particular book or text.

In brief, selections from the reading material of 200 to 300 words are taken from a suitable book and a series of questions on each passage prepared. These can be made to represent some rationale if required, so that various kinds of comprehension skills can be tested. A list of words from the materials may be selected so that oral word recognition skill can be covered as well as oral passage reading. The testing procedure may also include silent reading comprehension and listening comprehension of further selections.

A pupil's performance will be classified in terms of Independent, Instructional or Frustrational reading. If the pupil shows he would be capable of reading the material without need of support or guidance from a teacher, i.e. for pleasure or private study, his reading is classified as *Independent*. If he shows slightly less mastery so that he would occasionally need teacher-help, i.e. the material is of appropriate difficulty on which to learn and develop reading skills, his reading is classified as *Instructional*. If he shows such difficulty that the material would be unsuitable for him to read on his own or as a basis for learning, his reading is said to be at the *Frustrational* level.

Numerical criteria for these levels, based on number of words correctly read and comprehension questions answered have been suggested by Johnson and Kress (1965) as follows:

	Oral Accuracy	Comprehension
Independent Level	99%	90%
Instructional Level	95%	75%
Frustrational Level	90% or less	50% or less

These criteria could be made more accurate by research, Powell (1968) for example, suggests the Instructional criteria are too strict. The teacher should certainly feel free to adjust them as proves necessary. In any case, the qualitative aspects of reading behaviour which are associated with each level are just as important. The value of the technique lies as much with the way it allows teachers to make observations of individual reading characteristics as with the 'numerical' criteria.

A further possibility which greatly enhances the usefulness of the IRI is to classify materials in terms of 'readability'. This is a method of assigning a 'reading age' for prose material on the basis of simple measures of comprehensibility such as sentence length and numbers of syllables. A useful introduction to the study of readability is provided by Gilliland's book *Readability* (1972).

A readability measure is a useful guide in selecting materials for an inventory in the first place. Further, a pupil's performance on an inventory of a known level of readability will give some idea of how he would cope with other materials of the same readability.

The literature on IRIs gives a much fuller discussion of the reading behaviours characteristic of each level than space allows for here and the teacher would be advised to consult a relevant text before using the technique. Johnson and Kress (1965) provide a very full description of the technique.

At the time of writing the value of attempting a simple assessment of attainment with the available standardized prose reading tests is open to doubt. The available tests all suffer from ageing of their norms. The *Neale Analysis of Reading Ability* dates from 1958, as does the prose reading section of Daniels and Diack's *Standard Reading Tests*. Schonell's *Simple Prose Reading Test R2* dates from the 1940s while the Durrell *Analysis of Reading Difficulty* has only US-based grade norms, though it is occasionally used in Britain.

Some of the above tests have considerable diagnostic value, but the

diagnostic procedures they embody — essentially analysis of oral
reading errors — can be practised equally well with any prose material —
hence the value of IRIs. The comprehension checks they embody tend
to be on the simple side and some teachers might find them less
searching than is required. In addition the tests tell the teacher little
about the pupil's ability to read any particular materials. The IRI has
the advantage of using the proposed teaching material as the context
for testing.

Sentence completion: vocabulary

One of the most widely used forms of testing is the sentence
completion task. Usually this involves the choice of a word (or phrase)
from a number of given alternatives so that a sentence can be
completed meaningfully: e.g.

I have lost my (thin; how; *dog*; at)

This technique has variously been described as testing 'reading
experience', vocabulary, and reading comprehension. Although we may
surmise that it tests all these things and more — very little research has
been conducted to determine empirically what exactly is being tested.

It may however be useful to briefly classify the apparent attributes
of the test task:

1. *Decoding*: To get more than a chance number of questions right
the reader would have to be able to decode most of the words in the
sentence, although perhaps not all. In the case of the easier items in the
tests this is often sufficient to select the correct answer. The simplicity
and commonplace nature of the language make it unlikely that all but
the most limited pupils would get the item wrong.

2. *Memory-span*: As sentences become longer the load on the
reader's word memory span increases. The tendency for longer
sentences to provide harder items suggests that this capacity is tested by
the item in the same way it is involved in normal sentence reading.
However the demands are less than those encountered in sustained
reading of a prose passage or longer units such as chapters of books,
where long-term memory powers are required for effective reading.

3. *Knowledge of linguistic structure*: Sometimes the answer choices
contain only one grammatically acceptable alternative. The reader must
therefore be sensitive to the structural constraints placed upon him.

The look-out saw the _____ crossing the bridge (slightly; *train*;
dangerous; foolish; miserable)

Here the correct choice is dictated by the grammatical nature of the sentence and distractors. Unfortunately test constructors have not studied the possible differences between items based on structure and those based on meaning, although a recent elaboration on the sentence-completion format, *The Wide-Span Reading Test*, does enable the tester to code wrong answers diagnostically on the basis of either semantic (Vocabulary) or syntactical (Linguistic) error.

4. *Reading Experience*: Reading tests cannot but reflect some kind of stylistic bias. In practice they usually reflect the language of books and of formal discourse. The language of such tests would be bafflingly alien to one not accustomed to the 'literary voice' of language: a reader lacking in reading experience might be able to decode the words and be untroubled by structure yet would be unable to select the appropriate answer. To the 'unread' all of the alternatives in the following might seem sensible:

With a rueful smile he at last _____ his mistake (*confessed*; concealed; denied; embodied)

5. *Social experience and factual information*: Items that have taken the form of factual statements or describe anything but the most banal aspects of experience are open to the accusation that they are testing things extraneous to reading. The bias towards middle class readers' experience in many tests is undeniable, but a completely culture-free test of reading would be difficult to produce. Similarly, it would be hard to test a pupil's vocabulary without simultaneously testing his general knowledge. Again, it has not been experimentally determined how far such factors really effect test results.

6. *Vocabulary*: That understanding of word meanings is involved in test performance has been implied in the preceding remarks. Easier items certainly use common vocabulary, while intermediate and more difficult items use words that are often longer and less common in daily speech and writing. It is, however, unlikely that success depends upon knowledge of every word in an item. One can speculate that use of structure and context may compensate for imperfect vocabulary knowledge. However, it is also likely that knowledge of precise meanings for the answer-choice is crucial in some items, particularly the more difficult items intended for the older secondary aged pupil.

7. *Use of context*: The choice of the correct word in many sentence-completion items rests finally on the way the testee is able to make use of the context. In practice most published sentence completion-tests exclude the structural cues from all but the easiest items. The child is thus confronted with a set of words which are all grammatically possible, but only one of which is contextually accept-

able. This may well involve both of the factors mentioned in 4) and 6). In other words, the reader must discriminate between the meaning of the words — a matter of vocabulary — and then on the basis of his reading experience judge which word would be contextually most appropriate. One may argue that these are skills called into play in fluent everyday reading, although the reader would of course have access to much more information, including that which lay outside any individual sentence.

It would be wrong to assume that all the above processes and skills are involved in any one item. Some times items are deliberately written to exclude a particular factor. For example, context and reading experience can be eliminated by presenting all the items as definitions:

A dog is a kind of (Animal; Alsatian; Plant; Complaint; Danger)

In the above item knowledge of word-meanings is the crucial factor and few of the other considerations we have mentioned are of any importance.

Sentence-completion tests have been widely employed for research and large-scale survey work, notably the surveys of national reading standards carried out periodically between 1938 and 1971. For such use they have the great advantage of providing a statistically reliable test which can be completed in a relatively short time. These qualities suit such tests to some educational purposes very well, particularly the screening of large numbers of pupils rapidly and reliably, prior to more intensive assessment of special groups. The technique also has value as a means of assessing the development of intermediate skills, where the reader is beginning to make use of contextual and linguistic cues and reading is becoming a matter of comprehension more than mechanics.

Continuous prose: comprehension

The use of continuous prose — and occasionally verse — as a basis for reading assessment is second in popularity to the sentence-completion task. Many of the attributes of the sentence-completion task discussed previously would be involved in the reading of longer passages. Also, it has yet to be demonstrated by research that sentence-completion and other vocabulary tasks test an attainment really distinct from prose-comprehension. The prose-comprehension does however have the virtue of being a closer approximation to 'real reading' and creates the possibility for a more intrinsically interesting reading test.

Comprehension sub-skills

A further possibility for the technique is that by careful wording of questions it is possible to test different facets of comprehension. This raises similar problems to those mentioned at the beginning of the chapter; there is by no means unequivocal evidence for the 'distinctness' of different comprehension factors. Most of the evidence is derived from research with American samples, often students in further and higher education.

Amongst the comprehension tests that do employ sub-scales there is a fairly consistent pattern of distinction between the global and inferential aspects of comprehension on the one hand, and the specific and detailed aspects on the other hand. Within these two major categories a proliferation of sub-scales may be found.

The fact that it is not possible to justify some of the distinctions between comprehension processes does not wholly invalidate tests which approach reading in this way. Some sub-scales may be reasonable guides for teaching — particularly remedial work, and particularly in the case of the occasional pupil who shows uneven performance across sub-tests. The problem of how great such differences need to be before one can attach any teaching significance to them can be tackled in a number of ways:

In the first place the difference in raw scores may be so great that the teacher can subjectively judge the difference to be significant. A more objective criterion involves appraising the scores in terms of their *standard errors* (see page 44). These indicate the limits within which one can assume a pupil's 'true' score on a single test lies. When this suggests the possibility of overlap between two or more scores the teacher should regard the seeming difference with suspicion. The mechanics of this procedure are described more fully in the subsequent section on profiles based on sets of whole test scores. An even more sophisticated alternative would be to establish the statistical correlation between the two sub-tests and then derive the 'predicted' scores for one sub-test on the basis of another. Where actual scores differed substantially from 'predicted' scores a genuine difference may be suspected. Such a technique is however more the province of the researcher than the class teacher — although the increasing availability of electronic calculating machines may alter this position. The reader who seeks a detailed review of research in comprehension sub-skills should consult Roger Farr's *Reading: What can be measured?* (1969).

It will suffice to say here that the sub-skills which have been identified have depended upon the particular methods used by the researchers and that findings are far from unanimous. However most studies have tended to find that some kind of word-meaning or vocabulary factor has been of outstanding importance and that any other skills identified have been relatively less significant. Those that have emerged tend to be of two types. One is a set of general, global and inferential forms of comprehension, while the other type consists of skills concerned with reading for specific or explicit points. In addition some kind of rate or speed of reading skill tends to emerge as an independent element of comprehension ability. The whole matter is however a confused one, as Roger Farr points out. In general the teacher would be advised to employ tests which most fairly reflect the pattern of skills he has been endeavouring to teach, but sub-test scores should be treated with great caution.

Multiple-choice and mechanical marking of comprehension

Nearly all the testing techniques mentioned employ a purely objective method of answering and marking. The correct answer has to be chosen from a finite set of alternatives (multiple-choice) or short written answers (usually one word) are required which leave little room for doubt about rightness and wrongness. Research in testing usually confirms that these methods are just as valid as those requiring fuller or more personal responses.

Two doubts tend to remain however. In the first place, teachers may find that this kind of answering affects children differently. Some will respond spuriously well to the particular task set and through this 'test sophistication' obtain inflated scores. Others (the more sensitive and thoughtful, some teachers claim) seem allergic to this rigid and mechanical situation, and thus fail to do themselves justice. Where typical groups of children are tested these two types of pupil will balance each other, so the group result is not affected. Where an individual child is being considered this problem cannot be so easily discounted. Interpretation of his performance should indeed take this into account and the use of more than one test — each with different testing formats — may be desirable.

The second doubt is perhaps more fundamental and concerns the way the use of relatively mechanical procedures distorts what is actually tested and tends to exclude many aspects of reading which are important, but not easily coaxed on to a test-paper. Some of these aspects of reading concern interest, enjoyment and habits in reading. Suggestions are made subsequently about how more might be done about this, but it is unfortunately the case that these all-important aspects of reading teaching are sometimes neglected simply because they cannot be easily tested. Apart from this, it sometimes seems that comprehension testing in particular does not lend itself to assessment of the more mature reader's response and understanding.

Certainly where the teacher's aims are more ambitious or literary a mechanical response system may violate the basic values which lie behind the teaching, as when *expression* of understanding or quality of personal judgement are valued. Such values are however often remote from teachers concerned with early or remedial teaching of reading where the need for objective assessment is greatest. The mechanical test further, has the advantage of isolating at least some aspects of comprehension so they can be observed largely independently of the pupil's expressive powers. In any case where the mechanical or objective comprehension test is employed as an intrinsic part of teaching and is combined with other forms of assessment these objections about 'reductionism' are less crucial. Tests, in the final analysis, are only one component in a well-rounded assessment of reading.

Cloze Tests

One of the few techniques for measurement of reading ability which has a thorough research and theoretical background is the 'cloze' technique. Since 1953 it has been widely used in reading research, both as a method of assessing the difficulty or 'readability' of prose material and — to a lesser extent — as a means of testing and researching reading ability. The technique involves deleting a given number of words from a passage of prose and then having pupils attempt to supply the words which have been deleted: In effect the cloze technique treats reading as a language process in which the reader pitches his linguistic resources and experiences against those of the reading material, for example:

The surface of water is _____ by a fine film. In fact all liquids have _____ films. They are stretched over the liquid like the _____ on an African drum. One experiment that can _____ done with this skin is to float a needle on water.

First, get a dry steel needle and a _____ of water. Place the needle on the prongs of a fork _____ lower the fork on to the _____ of the water. _____ the fork is then gently taken away the needle will _____ . The same trick can be done _____ razor blades.

For most experimental work it has sufficed to delete words at random and score as correct only responses providing the exact word deleted. Experimentally it has been shown that allowing equally sensible alternatives does not alter the results significantly but makes more work for the test-marker. However for educational testing it is clearly desirable that alternative answers — providing they are really equally appropriate — should be permitted.

When someone reads fluently they certainly do not have to 'read' every word in the material. Many words will only be seen peripherally, others will not be seen at all. In effect fluent reading is such an efficient process that only a portion of the information contained in the passage has to be used for full comprehension. It follows that if some words were actually left out the effect of their loss would be slight, indeed the reader would probably be able, if asked, to supply the missing matter for himself. The efficiency with which one could do this is a sign, not only of how easy or hard the passage was, but how good the reader is.

Figure 4A: A Cloze test passage, attempted by an 11-year-old boy.

The surface of water is covered by a fine film.
In fact all liquids have fine films. They are stretched over the liquid like the canvas on an African drum. One experiment that can be done with this skin is to float a needle on water.

First, get a dry steel needle and a bowl of water. Place the needle on the prongs of a fork. and lower the fork on to the surface of the water. after the fork is then gently taken away the needle will float . The same trick can be done with razor blades.

The original words were: covered; such; skin; be; bowl; then; surface; if; float; with.

It may seem strange that people should seem to 'know' what a writer has written, without the word being there! However the structured and lawful nature of language makes it possible to do this on the basis of probability. For example, the probability of a marker such as 'the' or 'an' coming before a noun is great, and the competent reader uses his knowledge of probabilities such as these in order to read efficiently. Similarly, if he has understood what he is reading up to a given place in the text the chances are he would not be dumbfounded by the loss of more important meaning-bearing words, such as nouns and verbs. Cloze procedure tests reading ability by presenting the pupil with problems just like these.

The cloze method thus seems to have great potential for valid and convenient group assessment of reading attainment. The research on cloze procedure has demonstrated its potential but much of this research was not carried out with a view to producing standardized and fully 'de-bugged' materials for teachers to use. Some tests have been published − for example the GAP and GAPADOL tests − however many questions about the use of cloze in attainment testing remain unanswered. Some suggestions for the use of the procedure as an informal means of diagnosis are given in Chapter Eight. The teacher who wishes to experiment with the method for himself should find that research articles on the subject will give many pointers to its application.

It must suffice here to mention the results of a piece of research by John R. Bormouth (1968), who has conducted extensive research on the cloze procedure. He found that a cloze score of about 44 per cent corresponds to the Instructional Level of the Informal Reading Inventory, while a score of 57 per cent correct corresponds to the Independent Level. In other words pupils would have to be able to supply about 57 per cent or more of deleted words if they were to be expected to take the unmutilated test passage away and read it without very much help or support from the teacher. However, provided their scores reached the 44 per cent level, the book might still be suitable for use in class with adequate support, guidance and interpretation by the teacher (Instructional Level). These criteria must of course be treated only as an approximation where they are to be applied in situations different from those of the original experiment, which was carried out with US children in fourth, fifth and sixth grades of the elementary school. British teachers may however take them as a guide.

Reading rate and speed

Speed or rate of reading is sometimes distinguished by test constructors as an area of attainment different from vocabulary and comprehension. Certainly there is some sense in assuming that the less able readers will tend to read more slowly and that one's effectiveness as a reader in many situations will depend on how quickly one can read. In fact the research evidence tends to show that measures of speed and rate of reading are relatively independent of other measures.

A distinction must however be made between mechanical rate and comprehension rate. The former relies on fluency of oral reading or upon the speed with which print is scanned, and leaves unanswered the question of how well the pupil understood or absorbed the material. Where the speed-test is accompanied by some check on comprehension, as it is in the *Neale Analysis of Reading Ability* or the *NFER's Secondary Reading Test EH-3* the results will have greater educational credibility. For example, the reader may be told to read a passage as quickly as possible, but in the course of doing so to underline the appropriate word from a set in brackets:

This is a simple test (of/in/at) speed reading which demonstrates the (prospect/method/helpless) of incorporating a simple check of the (reader's/rope's/riddle's) comprehension of the test passage.

Such tests do not necessarily assess the reader's ability to *judge* what pace of reading is appropriate for any particular situation, and indeed reading flexibility — the ability to read at an appropriate rate — is a neglected area of both teaching and testing.

Attitudes and reading habits

There are probably many cases of reading failure who escape notice in conventional attainment testing; readers who can read but reject the material supplied in school in preference for less approved reading matter. Alternatively they may engage in no voluntary reading at all, although this total rejection is perhaps rarer than teachers sometimes believe.

A difference between backward readers and reluctant readers can sometimes be distinguished and a teacher may suspect that the proportions in the latter group are sufficiently great to merit some attempt to assess them. Certainly a pupil's attitude to books may be at odds with his capacity to read them, yet ultimately it is attitude and habit that judge the success of a teacher's efforts. In some situations attainment test results may conceal as much as they reveal and the inclusion of information about attitude and habit might make for a much more accurate impression about the state of reading.

The study of attitudes to books and reading, and actual reading habits has traditionally been the preserve of the researcher. There are no published materials at present available for the teachers for this kind of assessment and the area is largely an unexplored one. There are some obvious difficulties in asking pupils to express (or give vent to) their attitudes in this way. Many teachers may feel that an informally gathered impression is all that is necessary or desirable. It may however be acceptable to conduct a more general type of inquiry in which only a random sample of pupils are involved or to confine the exercise to a relatively factual inquiry about number of books read, membership of public libraries, purchase of own books, and so on. In spite of the special problems associated with this approach, the authors feel it is one which deserves much more serious consideration. A survey of *what* children read is just as legitimate a way of examining 'standards' as a survey of *how* they read and might raise equally serious and provocative questions about a school's work in teaching reading.

The two main objective methods which could be used — the attitude scale and the questionnaire — are briefly described below. Before experimenting with their own versions, however, teachers should consult a fuller text such as Oppenheim's *Questionnaire Design and Attitude Measurement* (1966).

Attitude Scales: 'Tests' of attitudes are commonly called 'scales' and usually consist of a series of statements about the subject under consideration. The person's attitude is indicated by the way he endorses each statement. Various question formats are possible. The person may be asked to simply indicate which statements he agrees/disagrees with or a more elaborate rating of statements on a five-point scale of agreement/disagreement may be employed. The methods could be adapted to apply to individual book titles on a like/dislike basis as well as reading tasks, library periods etc.

Questionnaires: A general impression of the standard and extent of reading activity in a school or class can be gained by use of questionnaires which involve the pupil in supplying factual information. This might deal with the number of books read, favourite titles of reading matter and library membership and use. Again the technique has limitations: there may be a discrepancy between reported and actual behaviour and the results may be more use in formation of general policy than in individual teaching. A further difficulty concerns the sheer bulk of information that can accumulate if one is not careful. This can be to some extent avoided if the questionnaire is limited to five or six well-worded questions and is then only applied to a representative sample of children. Where the concern about the cultural responsibilities of teaching reading is great enough, however, the exercise could be worth the trouble.

Profiles of attainment

The idea of producing a diagnostic profile based on scores from a number of different tests or sub-tests attracts many teachers. We have already raised doubts about the possibility that any differences between the various aspects of reading ability can be genuinely measured by existing tests. Nevertheless if the teacher is prepared to undertake the additional expense and labour involved, this approach still has some justification. There is always the chance of finding some individual discrepancies with teaching implications, although they will almost certainly occur in only a small minority of cases. For example, a pupil may perform well in tasks of mechanical reading and word recognition while having very little comprehension power. Similarly one may wish to distinguish between poor comprehenders who are able to read at a satisfactory rate, and those who comprehend poorly just because their rate is exceptionally slow.

Differences between test scores

The genuineness of any apparent differentials between test scores depends on the length of the tests involved; sub-tests in particular may be so short that meaningful comparisons cannot be made.

More technically thorough test manuals report a *standard error of measurement* (SEm) by means of which an approximate statistical interpretation can be made of any apparent score differences. It is acceptable to interpret the standard error of measurement so as to be 95 per cent certain that a pupil's 'true' score lies in a band or corridor from two standard errors below his obtained score to two standard errors above his obtained score. When obtained scores have standard errors attached to them and the corridors do not overlap, the difference can be expected to be genuine in 95 per cent of cases. When there is an overlap, the difference cannot really be taken to be significant. In the example on the following page we can see that while two pupils both had higher scores for comprehension than for rate, only in the case of the second pupil do the standard errors allow us to assume with any confidence that the difference is real.

Comprehension Test SEm = 1.75
Rate Test SEm = 1.0

Pupil A	*Pupil B*
1. Comprehension score = 104	1. Comprehension score = 107
2. Rate score = 100	2. Rate score = 95

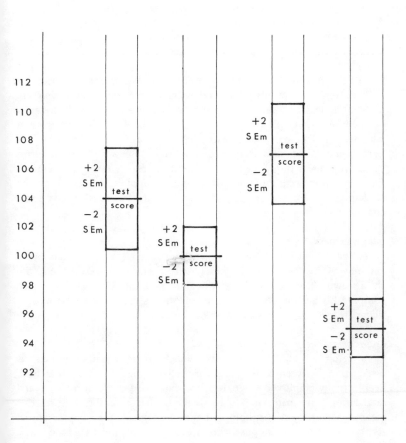

This technique is strictly only applicable to groups of scores, but a
teacher could use it for informally evaluating differences in individual
pupils' performances.

Chapter Five

Backward readers

One of the most important uses of objective tests is in the identification — screening — of pupils who need special attention because they are performing less well than their peers i.e. backward readers. There are a bewildering variety of ways in which this can be done, depending upon whether one is concerned with screening out the 'illiterate', the 'semi-literate', the 'slow learner' or the 'underachiever'. All these forms of backwardness imply slightly different types of testing procedures. Each criterion and the kind of testing it implies will be discussed subsequently. First, however, the term 'backwardness' needs some comment.

Backwardness

To be backward, a pupil must be reading less well than other children of his own age. In nearly all criteria of backwardness, the child's own chronological age is the starting point. The next stage is to compare his performance with that of other children of the same age. There are two main ways this may be done:

1. Backwardness in reading age

A criterion of backwardness, which is sometimes applied, is discrepancy between reading and chronological age. Criteria which have been actually employed range from less than one year to over two years' retardation. This criterion has the weakness that it has different relative meaning at different chronological ages, as explained in Chapter Three. As the number of pupils who are a year or more behind their chronological age in reading age may well increase with age, the criterion becomes an increasingly stringent one. Consequently, more children will be classified as backward by a secondary school screening procedure than by a junior school one. There is no necessary objection to this being allowed to happen, as it would be due to an increasing tendency for less able readers to reach a standstill in development of reading skill, or at least to make progressively less ground. The need for remedial help is thus a real one.

A reading age may be divided by the child's chronological age and the result multiplied by 100 to give a reading *quotient*. The average child would get a quotient score of 100 in this way, those below average would get less than 100, while those above average would get 100+. There is no real advantage in doing this, however, because the quotient makes it no clearer *how* backward (or advanced) a child is relative to other pupils. Would a quotient of 85 at seven years be a sign of severe backwardness? It is not possible to tell very precisely as we have no idea how many other seven-year-olds tend to have a quotient of 85. All we know is that it represents a year's backwardness at this age, while it represents a greater amount at nine years. It may well be the case that relatively more children will have quotients of 85 and below at nine years, so relatively speaking the nine-year-old with a quotient of 85 would be less backward than the seven-year-old. If a teacher wants to know how well a pupil reads for his age quotients should be used with caution, particularly if he then proceeds to compare children of different ages.

The great disadvantage of the Reading Age criterion of backwardness is that it is often impossible to estimate in advance what proportion of children are likely to be picked out by any given criterion of retardation. All we know is that the greater the discrepancy criterion, the fewer children are likely to be identified. The teacher or administrator has to decide in advance what a minimal level of acceptable attainment would be and hope that the numbers who fall short of it are not overwhelming.

2. Backwardness in standardized score units

It has already been explained in Chapter Three, that a standardized score expresses a pupil's performance in terms of the proportion of other pupils that do worse or better. A standardized score of 85 means that the pupil is in the bottom 16–17 per cent of his age group. This relative proportional meaning remains the same regardless of the chronological age of the pupil in nearly all tests which are standardized in this way. This system is to be recommended, not only for its precision, but for its consistency.

Illiteracy and semi-literacy

These terms are in daily use and may be used to describe adults or teenagers, who do not read and write as well as someone feels they should. The term is, however, vague; it is not unknown for university professors to describe their students as illiterate! In general, they are rarely used of the young child, who is still learning to read.

Illiteracy has been defined as being at or below the reading level of a typical seven-year-old, while semi-literacy is represented by the standards of average children between seven and nine years of age. The standards of seven- and nine-year-olds have probably risen since 1938, which has been taken as the anchor-point criterion. Even the survey in 1970/1[1] had difficulty in reaching a single satisfactory criterion.

By 1938's standards, few of the children tested were illiterate, but there remained, by definition, a group of bottom scorers, who were clearly less literate than most of their age peers.

Slow learners and underachievers

Any reading test will reveal that not all children read equally well. Chapter Two described in detail how reading ability tends to be distributed about a mean or median point. There will always be some children who are reading far below the majority of their age group.

Some psychologists think, however, that this extreme group is made up of two different types of children. Some are there because of basic limitations in their mental ability (slow learners), while others are performing well below their mental 'potential' (underachievers).

Slow Learners: The slow learner, it is claimed, is already reading as well as he can be expected to do. Although his reading age is low in relation to his chronological age, it is as high as he can be expected to make it in view of his low basic intelligence. Although such a pupil will need special teaching which is suited to slow pace of learning, it may be unrealistic in aiming to raise his reading to a level much above average.

Underachievers: These pupils may also have low reading ages relative to chronological age. However, their intelligence test scores show that mentally they are average, or even above average. These children are the 'could do betters'. The problem for the teacher, it is argued, is to tackle the pupil's learning by looking for particular weaknesses or specific difficulties and working on these. The causes of underachievement would merit a book in their own right. They certainly include social, cultural and emotional factors as well as specific mental blocks (specific learning difficulties). The problems of assessing these latter types of difficulty are discussed in Chapter Eight. An underachiever might have a Reading Age in excess of the chronological age, but still seem to be reading below potential — this kind of case is however in practice of less concern to teachers.

There are dangers in these two ideas. The former can be used to write off a child as doomed to near-illiteracy, and the latter can tempt teachers into exerting too much pressure on a child.

---

1   K.B. Start and B.K. Wells, *The Trend of Reading Standards*, 1972, pp. 49—55.

If these two concepts are to be used constructively teachers should be confident on the one hand that the number of children who are of such low intelligence that they cannot learn to read is very small and on the other that it is the right approach, rather than sheer pressure, which will be used to help the underachiever.

Reluctant Readers: This expression is sometimes confused with the term 'backward readers', but it refers primarily to children who seem able to read, but are unwilling to do so. Such children are not identified by testing, but by the subjective judgements of their teachers or parents. It is important to ensure that a child's professed lack of interest in reading does not conceal an inability to read — as one suspects it does for many so-called 'reluctant readers'.

Use of intelligence tests

From the preceding discussion, it will be clear that intelligence testing is an important aspect of the assessment of the backward reader. The crucial question is how valid such tests are as a guide to how well a child should be reading. The subject has a long research background and is still controversial.

Draw a man tests

The simplest means of assessing a child's mental development — a term which is usually taken as synonymous for intelligence — is the 'Draw a Man' Test. This was devised by F.L. Goodenough in 1926 and has its origin in the notion that 'a child draws what he knows, rather than what he sees'. The children are therefore asked to draw a man and awarded marks for the inclusions of limbs, facial detail, fingers, etc. and for showing these features in the correct positions and proportions; in all there are 51 points in the scale. The original test was used widely for many years and there is considerable evidence for its validity, based on comparisons with other intelligence tests and teacher's ratings as well as Goodenough's own results. Artistic ability is shown to be practically negligible as far as influencing the score is concerned.

In 1963 the test was substantially revised and restandardized on a large sample of American children aged 5—15 by D.B. Harris. He added a 'Draw a woman' scale and an experimental Self Drawing scale and extended the 'Draw a man' scale. The new standardization gives scores in terms of deviation from the mean rather than IQ based on considerations of mental age. The test is easy to administer and marking, although involved, is systematic and has been shown to be consistent for different markers. Full details of the revised test together with background information not given in the test manual are included in Harris (1963). The test itself is available in Britain from NFER Publishing Company. The technique has been applied in the assessment of reading readiness, but whether it can be used to measure reading potential throughout the age and ability range is open to question.

Non-verbal reasoning tests

Many general tests of intelligence available to teachers are of the pencil and paper type and present 'verbal reasoning' problems in written form. These are, however, inappropriate for pupils who are weak at reading. A test of a pupil's mental powers through exclusively non-verbal media is, therefore, often used. Most frequently used for this purpose are the *Raven's Progressive Matrices*; *Raven's Coloured Matrices* and the *NFER Non-Verbal Tests*. Characteristically, these tests present logical problem solving situations. These require the use of rational capacities in situations which are largely free of any language or reading load. The test items make extensive use of abstract and geometrical designs.

For the younger pupil the problems may be posed in pictorial form, as in the NFER *Picture Intelligence Tests*. Pupils who show non-verbal ability substantially higher than their reading attainment may be designated 'underachievers'. Certainly children of this kind are often identified. However it does not follow that the teaching which is applied will always result in a successful improvement in reading to the level of non-verbal ability. Experimental efforts in this direction have been largely disappointing.

Verbal and non-verbal reasoning ability are thought to be separate aspects of intelligence. The latter may indicate potential for performance on problems which are free of verbal components, rather than in linguistically-loaded school subjects. Non-verbal performance may indicate that a pupil has certain intellectual worth despite his poor reading, but it does not follow that reading or many other school situations allow for the application of such ability. Certainly it is the verbal reasoning test which usually features in research on the prediction of academic success. There may thus be less reason for thinking a language-based skill such as reading can be predicted from performance on pictorial and non-linguistic tasks than is often assumed.

Reading-free intelligence tests

It is possible, using oral administration, to assess a non-reader's intellectual ability in verbal tasks. Typical of such tests are Young's *Non-Reader's Intelligence Test* in which the questions are read out by the teacher and the pupil records his answer on a multiple-choice answer sheet, and the *English Picture Vocabulary Test* in which the pupil indicates his understanding of dictated words by choosing the appropriate picture in a set of four.

The use of a linguistic testing medium makes it more likely that test

Figure 5A

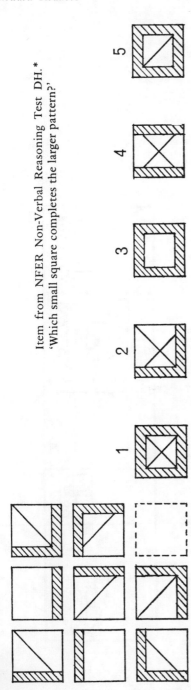

Item from NFER Non-Verbal Reasoning Test DH.*
'Which small square completes the larger pattern?'

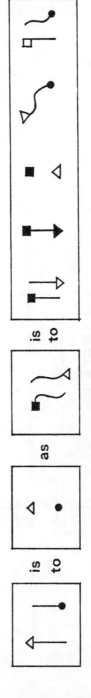

Item from NFER Non-Verbal Reasoning Test BD.*
'Which shape has the same relationship to the third as the second has to the first?'

* Reproduction of these items has been done only with the express permission of the NFER Publishing Company Ltd.

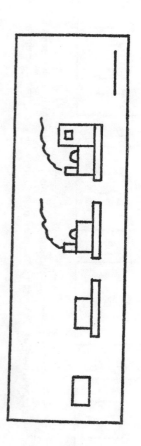

Item from NFER Picture Test A.*
'Which train completes the sequence?'

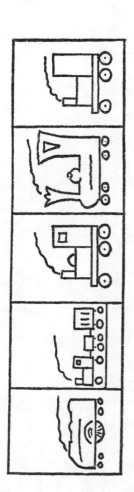

performance will relate to reading potential. However it is as yet not clear that the verbally bright poor reader has any greater chance of eventual success than the less bright. The value of the distinction between dull pupils and underachievers certainly lies less in the way it can shape teachers' expectations in the long-term and more in the way it enables them to be more sensitive and appropriate in their day-to-day approach to the pupils.

Intelligence tests may also be useful in the assessment of pupils in the general remedial context where progress in all school subjects is unsatisfactory. It must be stressed however that group tests available to teachers are less precise about an individual child than the individual tests employed by educational psychologists. Poor performance on a group test in school may be due to any number of extraneous factors, particularly in the case of the backward reader or remedial pupil who may come to the test with a built-in sense of failure.

Mis-classifications

It has been stressed that a test score is an estimate rather than a statement of fact. The parameters of a pupil's likely true standing can be estimated by considering the relative reliability of a test and the standard error to be attached to scores. Even a highly reliable test will classify pupils as semi-literate or in need of remedial help who would, on another occasion, have just exceeded the criterion score. Simultaneously, some pupils will elude classification when in fact they fall below the criterial level. The use of a battery of two or more tests will help reduce such chance errors, and other criteria, such as teachers' recommendations, can give perspective to test results. The point is that while a standardized test is a valuable screening technique it cannot hope to be 100 per cent accurate.

Time factors

It has already been pointed out that age norms for tests apply most accurately to the time of year at which the original sample was tested. A test which was standardized on nine-year-olds at the end of the school year will probably apply too stringent a standard to children tested at the beginning of the year. Although the beginning of a year is the most sensible time for screening test constructors are not always able to carry out their standardizations at this time and accordingly test manuals should be read carefully so the teacher has some idea about what time of year the standard applies to.

The effects of testing pupils at the end of the school year, and then applying the results in the following school year — possibly in a new school — should be mentioned.

Where a reading age scale is employed such a practice has certain weaknesses. The weak readers will at best remain static over time, perhaps actually regressing. On the other hand the abler pupils will probably continue to increase in their reading age, so that the overall pattern of ability alters over the holiday period. A similar effect will be obtained with standardized scores, where the age-adjustment system will probably penalize the weaker readers so that if re-tested their summer scores will appear optimistic.

When to screen?

As has been suggested, screening is most fruitful at the beginning of a school year, provided pupils have had sufficient time to settle in a new class or new school. However the question arises as to when in a school career screening should be carried out. Logically enough, times of transfer are usually the occasion for screening, and it is desirable for the inducting school to carry this out because of the time factors mentioned previously. It is also important that pupils are screened periodically rather than just once. The experience of surveys and test-standardization shows that pupils who at one age are reading at a satisfactory level may in a year or two lose their impetus and become candidates for remedial help. For example, a pupil who has mastered the mechanics of reading to the satisfaction of infant or early junior teachers may fail to acquire or consolidate the more sophisticated skills required for top junior work. The transition from lower secondary work to examination course reading requirements probably give rise to a similar 'jolt'.

Pre-reading

It is not proposed to say very much about the screening of children at entry into infant and first schools as the role of standardized tests is limited. Certain important functions as screening for auditory and visual defects are necessary as a prelude to the learning of reading — but these are more properly the province of the school medical service.

Opinions are divided on the concept of reading readiness and readiness testing. Where such screening is thought necessary a simple observational schedule or checklist may be found more appropriate than a test. Such techniques are a topic in their own right. Many of the texts on reading readiness include examples of schedules of this kind — such as one proposed by Schonell and described by Downing and Thackray (1971) in *Reading Readiness*. Dean and Nichols in their book *Framework for Reading* (1974) describe a checklist scheme of reading assessment. This not only covers many aspects of pre-reading skills and development, but goes on to comprehensively deal with formal reading skills. Also, some psychological services who employ their own schedules may make them generally available, such as the *Croydon*

Check List and *Guidelines for Teachers.*[1]

A brief discussion of readiness tests is found in Chapter Seven where they are included because of their potential as diagnostic instruments applied in individual cases, rather than as a general screening device.

The notion that young children can be simply divided into the 'ready' and 'unready' on the basis of a test result is in any case a gross over-simplification. Downing and Thackray (1971) provide a fuller discussion of this point. A further problem with readiness tests is the way they are validated; the usual criterion is a child's score on a reading test given some time after formal reading teaching has begun. This is rather circumstantial evidence. A more reasonable form of validation would be to assess the effectiveness of the readiness test as a guide for the provision of effective teaching. This aspect of such tests is usually left unexplored by their constructors.

'At risk'

An expression which is sometimes used instead of reading readiness is that of a child being 'at risk'. This is a loose term, but is generally taken to mean that although the child has not yet failed in reading his present circumstances suggest that this is a genuine danger. Adverse social, cultural and familial conditions are indicators of an 'at risk' child, but test results may contribute to the picture. Readiness tests may well be included in this. Just as some children who fail reading readiness tests go on to have no difficulty in learning to read, there are 'at risk' children who defy the odds and learn to read without difficulty. The point to remember is that readiness and 'at risk' are only indicators of the *probability* of reading difficulty, derived from studies of large numbers of children. They have the advantage of objectivity, but disregard all the unique aspects of an individual case which the teachers are in a position to observe and should strive to become aware of.

Infant to junior transfer

Considerable importance is attached to the acquisition of initial reading skills in the early years of schooling. Any pupils who have failed to learn to read satisfactorily by the time they transfer from the first or infant school need to be identified so that remedial action can be taken.

A number of standardized tests are available for screening at seven plus and there is no question about their general effectiveness for the purpose. At the same time it would be as well to consider some of the difficulties that can arise, particularly if screening is carried out during

---

1 *Check List and Guidelines for Teachers No. 1* by Trevor Bryans and Sheila Wolfendale, Reading and Language Development, London Borough of Croydon (1973).

the infant years, rather than later in the first junior years.

It is unrealistic to expect infant age pupils to concentrate for long periods on pencil-and-paper group tests. For this reason few tests give norms for pupils below 7:0 years — those that do may well base their 'younger' norms on estimation of younger pupils' performance rather than direct testing. It is also extremely important to ensure that norms for tests do apply to top *infants* rather than first year *junior*. Norms for the latter will tend to be too stringent as they include the effects of teaching which has gone on in the first term or so of the junior year.

Test scores at this age may be subject to biases associated with the methods, materials and schemes used in the initial teaching phase. For example, a particular test, perhaps unintentionally, may favour the vocabulary and structures of a particular teaching scheme. At the same time teachers are so varied in the extent to which they adhere to set schemes that tests based purposefully on particular schemes would be no less subject to bias.

These difficulties are likely to be less acute when dealing with children transferring from first to middle schools. Other problems may replace them. In particular there are as yet no tests specifically developed for this purpose, or with norms based directly upon the performance of children following the first to middle school pattern. At present children entering middle schools have to be assessed on norms derived very largely from samples of younger junior children. This practice overlooks the possibility of differences in standards due to differences in the two systems.

Transfer to secondary school

Secondary schools dealing with unselective intakes often wish to know the relative reading standard of pupils. They may also require some notion of the range of reading ability in the intake and of the size of the group needing remedial help. Such checking will be necessary even when junior schools operate vigorous remedial programmes; poor attendance, and frequent illness are just two unavoidable causes of persistent reading backwardness. Many schools thus have to be prepared to deal with backwardness in reading, and a screening test is a necessary first step in determining the proportions of the problem.

It is at this stage that the problems associated with conveniently testing backward readers within a larger group containing average and advanced readers arise. An examination of the content of tests intended for 12-year-olds in general may reveal that it is too taxing for the less able in this age range. This is perhaps difficult to avoid in constructing a test intended to reflect the ability range of the general population. It seems absurd therefore to apply such a test for screening, particularly to teachers of classes which contain a substantial proportion of less able readers. There is some justice in this criticism. It is rarely however the purpose of screening to identify high-level readers, nor is it always of great importance to discriminate between even the average and above average reader. In fact it is by no means necessary for the test to produce a 'normal' distribution of scores. Screening can thus be carried out using a test which will be sufficiently easy to permit the weaker readers to show their paces. This can be done by selecting a test intended for a somewhat younger age group. As a result many of the abler children will probably do 'too well' so that their scores are close together at the ceiling imposed by the absence of any taxing items. This bias towards easier items will however lead to a conveniently magnified picture of any differences within the group of weaker readers. An 'age-appropriate' test would bunch together the weak and the very weak pupils in a range of a few marks; the 'younger' test would pick out the pupils in this group, as the slightly better pupils would now have more chance to show their relative superiority over the very weakest.

Such a procedure permits the fullest possible stratification of the potential remedial group so that sub-groups can be formed to give teaching at the appropriate level. The difference achieved by this second approach is represented in slightly exaggerated form in Figure 5C.

By such a procedure the possibility of giving scores a norm-referenced value is lost. However the backward 12-year-old's score may well earn a 10-year-old a standardized score of 100 — it is thus average for 10-year-olds and has an 'age-equivalence' of 10 years.

It is sometimes necessary for all the pupils in a year group to be initially given a test providing standardized scores. The 'younger test' process can be employed subsequently on smaller groups who have already been simply identified by the general screening test.

With younger children 'easier' tests may not be available in published form. The teacher may employ a simple test of her own construction but it is worth bearing in mind that some published tests already possess excellent discrimination properties amongst less advanced readers. The *Gates-McGinitie Primary Reading Test, Primary A* (British Standardization) for example, provides very fine discrimination amongst below average readers at seven plus, although it was actually standardized for the full range of ability in this same age group (see page 43).

The best that a conventional standardized test can be expected to do is help teachers begin to come to grips with the remedial situation. It is thus a guide to the nature of the problem not a prescription for its solution. There is no point in employing a sophisticated testing programme if follow-up action is not equally adequate. Unfortunately

Figure 5C: Distribution of raw scores on a test which spreads out the less able but is 'too easy' for average and more able readers

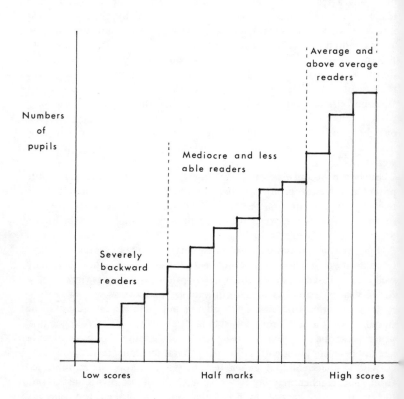

testing is perhaps the most simple step in the whole operation and it is only a single stage in the process. From then on precise and standardized equipment may either be unavailable or simply inappropriate.

Chapter Six

Measurement of progress

There are numerous non-test ways in which a teacher may decide a child or class has progressed or improved. However, it is important that if tests are to be used to measure improvement, then the rules which govern the interpretation of test scores are applied. The most effective statistical techniques involve the use of 'significance tests' (a useful explanation of the simpler tests is provided by A.C. Crocker in *Statistics for the Teacher*, 1974.) These tests involve a certain amount of computation and in practice teachers rarely apply them. However there is still value in being familiar with their workings even if they are not applied.

It has already been stressed that the assessment of reading should be a continuing process. A single testing exercise may indicate 'how far' a pupil has come since his education began, but it will leave many questions unanswered. As well as enabling the progress of each child to be monitored continuously, repeated testing can provide the teacher with valuable feedback on his own effectiveness. It is not only the pupil who is arousing special concern because of his backwardness who can benefit from a longitudinal programme of testing, and for this purpose, many school record cards allow for the multiple recording of test scores for their pupils. Continuous monitoring of progress, however, is not the concern solely of the more senior teacher concerned with administration. The following remarks are intended also to be relevant to the class teacher who will wish to follow the progress of his pupils over relatively short periods.

Repeated use of the same test

The simplest form of monitoring is that carried out in the course of teaching, when pupils may be tested from time to time on one particular test. For example, an increase in the number of words recognized on a Graded Word Recognition Test may be taken as an indication of progress.

The drawbacks of this sort of procedure are obvious, apparent progress may be the result of practice at the particular words, or of the pupil's overhearing when others are tested. Neither can a practice effect be ruled out on more sophisticated or complex reading tests, for on a second testing occasionally a pupil may be faced with passages upon which he has already worked in considerable detail. An 'improved performance' would be likely even if no overall progress in reading had been made.

In addition, where the standard error of a test is not known, it is impossible to assess the extent to which an apparent improvement may be due to the same random variations to which all mental measurement is prone. As has already been mentioned the standard errors of tests using only reading ages are rarely known. The teacher can rarely tell whether an increase in reading age is probably genuine — particularly if it is relatively small.

Equivalent forms

One way of overcoming the problem of practice effect is to use two equivalent or alternative forms of a test. Such forms are produced by giving two tests containing closely matched items to the same pupils and checking that any individual's relative standing on one test is equal to that on the other test. Perfect agreement between the two forms is never achieved, but nevertheless the two tests should be very highly correlated so we can assume they are both measuring the same thing.

Clearly a more general practice effect may still occur, and as in the case of a single test, some further analysis and interpretation is required to confirm an apparent improvement. Important factors which should be considered are the length of time between test sessions and the magnitude of the 'improvement' compared to the standard errors of the tests (this is discussed in a later section).

The age-adjustment given in standardized score tables helps to compensate for improvements in performance which are due entirely to maturation or a normal rate of learning rather than special effort or attention. The conversion tables may, as in the case of the *Wide-Span Reading Test*, include an adjustment for improvement due to repeated testing. Some more sophisticated checks are possible but they are more pertinent when the teacher wishes to evaluate some special improvement. Where general progress and the maintenance of standards are of concern there is less need to apply them.

Continuity of test forms

The development of reading is such that certain forms of test tasking are only appropriate at certain levels of development. Word-recognition, for example tends to be less important after the age of eight, and may be replaced by an increasing concern with silent-reading and comprehension. This in turn may be replaced by a growing concern with more flexible and efficient application of reading as a tool, and perhaps ultimately with the development of literary discernment and taste. Even where a particular test format or test task is sufficiently versatile to lend itself to testing across a wide range of age and ability, considerations of length call for the use of successive separate tests. These tests will be based on different samples at different age levels, thus they cannot be compared directly. However, a standardized score of 105 on a test for seven- to eight-year-olds indicates the same relative standarding as a standardized score of 105 on a test for nine- to ten-year-olds — i.e. a percentile equivalent of 64.3 at both ages. Accordingly, fully standardized tests which use compatible score systems are not entirely unrelatable. Similarly where two tests use the same format for at least some sub-sections (e.g. the successive stages of the *Edinburgh Reading Tests* or the same test task, as in NFER Sentence Reading Tests, A, AD, BD and EH—I, there are a good *à priori* grounds for believing that progress is being measured continuously along a single dimension. If there is a transition from one type of test to another the assumption of continuity is more suspect; it may not be proven that distinctly different aspects of attainment are being tested but an element of doubt about comparability will justifiably remain.

Long term monitoring

A particular test may be adopted to serve as a constant yardstick for the assessment of successive groups of pupils — particularly new intakes to a school, and in this way any changes in the standards of successive intakes or in the patterns of ability amongst the pupils can be observed. Such information is most often required for administrative purposes; however, individual teachers may also wish to have a constant reference point against which to assess successive year groups, or the different groups and types of pupils encountered during a teaching career.

However, the English language is subject to change over time; words or expressions which are common in one decade may be much less so in the rest, and they will be replaced by previously infrequent or non-existent usages. All tests which use language suffer from ageing effects. As their difficulty varies over time the norms must be regularly reviewed if a test's value as a measuring instrument is not to become suspect. For example, in 1974 the Scottish Council of Educational Research carried out a restandardization of the Burt Graded Word Reading Test which showed that words such as 'Refrigerator', 'Encyclopaedia' and 'Emergency' were much easier than when the test was originally constructed, while 'Glycerine', 'Melancholy' and 'Perambulating' were more difficult. In practice the constancy of a yardstick is elusive, particularly as the time-scale increases; many of the influences, such as changes in language itself, are very difficult to observe.

Regression

When the same group of pupils is tested on two occasions, some of the weaker pupils may appear to improve on the second occasion. Simultaneously some of the better pupils may seem to do worse. This effect can occur even if no instruction has been given in the intervening period, and is known as 'regression to the mean'. It is a side effect of the test's relative unreliability. As has already been explained, test scores are really estimates of a pupil's standing and a score value has a margin of error and fluctuation attached to it. For statistical reasons, the chance factors which cause this are most keenly felt at the two extremes of the score range of a test. The odds against exceptionally high or low scores are always relatively strong and the overall tendency is for scores to cluster about the mean. The more extreme a pupil's score, the greater the chance a subsequent score will be less extreme. A pupil who does really badly on a test could 'hardly do worse' on a second occasion, and it is very easy for an outstandingly good child to 'drop the odd mark' on the second occasion.

Regression is most obtrusive in practice when the progress of remedial pupils is being monitored. Where a remedial teacher finds apparent improvements in weak readers the possibility of a regression effect should be considered. The greater the time lapse between the two testing periods and the more substantial the remedial teaching efforts have been, the less likely it is that improvement is due solely to regression. Where there has been visible improvement in the reader's capabilities the improved test score can be treated as confirmatory and can place a normative value upon this improvement. If the test score itself is the only sign of improvement, and is in any case only slightly higher, a more sceptical interpretation may well be justified.

Some tests are less prone to regression than others, either because of the actual content of the tests, or because of its high reliability. It is however a danger to which teachers should be alerted.

Assessment of improvement

When a researcher wishes to evaluate a possible improvement in performance he will probably include all kinds of checks and controls that will eliminate the possibility that improvement is due to regression or other extraneous effects. Teachers however are not researchers, and the question arises as to whether practical conditions and circumstances make it possible for them to make any reasonable evaluation of progress and improvement.

There certainly are a number of measures that teachers can take without going to impractical extremes. In any case, it must be realized that while on the one hand research methods do provide stringent conditions for evaluating progress, the statistical tools of the researcher can also provide an over-lax criterion of effectiveness; a change which appears to be statistically significant is not necessarily an educationally significant or satisfactory one. The techniques to be described following are thus not a substitute for the teacher's own observations so much as a check or verification of them.

Multiple testing

The difference between two single test scores is a basic criterion of improvement. Where large numbers of pupils are tested it is fairly satisfactory, but a distinctly fairer picture can be obtained if *more than one* test score is involved on each occasion. An average score can be obtained for each testing session, and the difference between the two sets of averages treated as the index of improvement. This has the advantage of cancelling out errors associated with single test scores, but may be a somewhat extravagant procedure in some circumstances and may simply be too demanding for less able pupils. There is still the chance of regression effects between the two means, although they are likely to be much slighter than with single test scores.

Use of the standard error

A second refinement which can be conveniently applied with single test scores is to relate increases to the standard error of the test. It will be recalled that this is a quantity which expresses how much a score can vary as a result of the test's imperfect reliability. In practice it means that only differences which are more than twice as large as the standard error of the test can be confidently regarded as real improvements.

This technique is usually only applicable where the same test is used on both occasions, or when the standard error has been given for two equivalent forms. Where the standard error is given, it can be usefully applied to whole groups of scores.

A histogram can be produced, like those in Figure 6A and 6B. In these scores have been classified in terms of the number of points of improvement or deterioration they represent. In 6A and 6B histograms for standardized score-based results are displayed. In 6A the majority of pupils show 'no change' while equal proportions show increases and decreases in score. As these scores are based on a test which included an adjustment for age we can assume that the pupils have maintained an 'average' rate of progress for their age. The standard error of this test was 2 points of standardized scores, and very few pupils show gains or losses larger than twice the standard error. In other words, the changes in most of the scores are probably a result of the imperfect reliability of

Figure 6A:

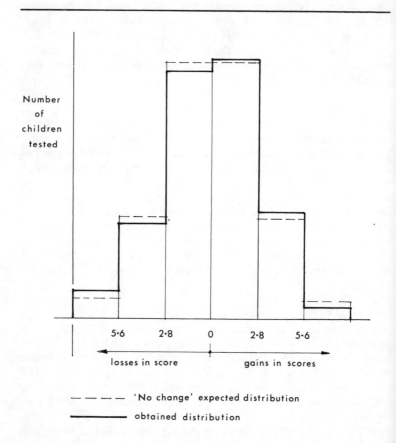

Number
of
children
tested

| 5·6 | 2·8 | 0 | 2·8 | 5·6 |

◄──────── losses in score   gains in scores ────────►

– – – – –   'No change' expected distribution
──────   obtained distribution

Figure 6B:

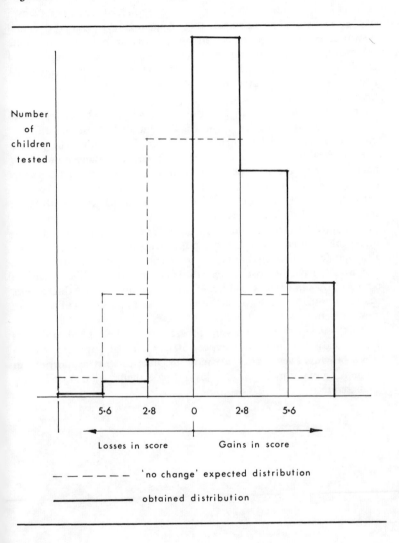

Number
of
children
tested

5·6   2·8   0   2·8   5·6

Losses in score   Gains in score

– – – – – –   'no change' expected distribution

——————   obtained distribution

the test, rather than to especial improvements of declines. A model such as that provided in Figure 6A can be produced for any test which has a known standard error (see Appendix A), and the actual distribution of change scores in any particular class group can be plotted against it. This can provide the teacher with a rough visual check on the extent to which satisfactory progress or improvement has been achieved. The greater the visual differences the greater the chance there has been improvement.

In Figure 6B an 'ideal' situation in which a great deal of actual improvement has occurred is shown. Few pupils have 'stood still' and most have scores higher than those obtained originally. The pattern suggests that this is a group of genuine improvers. Many more pupils have scored in the gain columns than would be expected by sheer chance fluctuations in score. In practice real scores will tend to form patterns which seem to deviate from either of the patterns displayed in these figures. In 6C, for example, there has been more improvement than found in Figure 6A, but it falls short of the rather dramatic ideal of Figure 6B — there are still some pupils who show decreases in score, although fewer than in the typical no change situation of 6A. Ideally one would make a statistical test to determine whether the difference between 6A and 6C was significant, or itself only a chance fluctuation. A simple visual check however, should of itself give some indication of improvement.

This visual method of assessing progress cannot be applied to reading ages so easily: although we expect 50 per cent of pupils to make a year's progress over a year, we have no guide to what proportions of children normally make more or less progress than this on most reading age based tests.

Figure 6C:

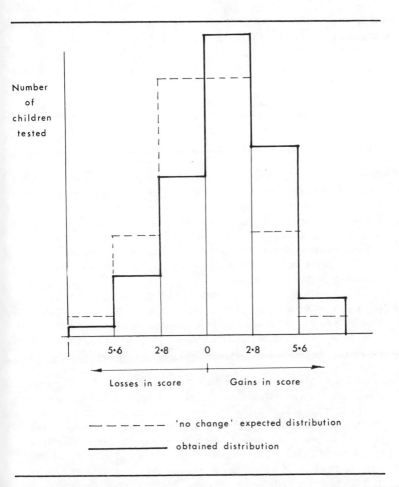

'no change' expected distribution

obtained distribution

Chapter Seven

Assessment of other language skills

This chapter deals with the problems and possibilities (there are more of the former than the latter) in assessing skills of language related to reading. Oracy, English, spelling and writing ability are all considered. While some kind of objective measurement is possible in all of these areas there is a long way to go in the development of test materials which can be conveniently used by teachers. Where test materials are available there is a tendency for them to be taken on trust and in ignorance of their limitations.

This is particularly true of spelling and English Language tests, where the user may be unaware of the extent to which much of the material fails to reflect current knowledge or practice. Many English specialists, particularly those in secondary schools, may feel that the image of English contained in an English test is either naive or completely irrelevant.

At the same time the claim that many secondary English specialists make for the 'unassessability' of their subject sometime seem too complacent. If teaching is effective, it must to some extent result in observable changes in the behaviour of pupils. Language itself is certainly a form of behaviour. It is behaviour which can be modified by teaching and individual development, and which can be observed. As we learn more about it we will become better able to observe and interpret it. Increased understanding may well lead to more appropriate and sensitive forms of measurement or observation. An example of the direction such work may take can be found in the research into writing which has been carried out by the Writing Research Unit at the London University Institute of Education. This has been concerned, amongst other things, with the pupil's 'sense of audience' in writing — his ability to use a style and tone appropriate for communication with his intended readership. A wide range of possible audiences exist, and the writer's flexibility in adapting to a particular audience may be a useful criterion of his writing ability. Such work is however a pointer to possible new forms of assessment — it is not a ready-made prescription.

Oracy

A certain level of skill in oracy — the ability to use and understand spoken language — is necessary for success in literacy — the ability to use and understand written language. It is therefore highly desirable to assess reading ability in the light of oral development; a pupil who displays poor comprehension of the spoken word cannot be expected to understand its written equivalent. Tests of listening vocabulary and comprehension to match their written counterparts would thus be useful. However, at the time of writing only the NFER's *Tests of Proficiency in English* employ this system. Here the tests of reading and listening use some identical material, so that any discrepancy between oral and written understanding can be observed.

These tests are however intended for use with young children and non-native speakers of English, and teachers of older junior and secondary pupils would have to use their own informal tests of listening. The user of any measure of listening comprehension should however be cautioned; although educationists have sometimes claimed that listening is a valid indicator of reading capacity there is no conclusive evidence for this. Discrepancies in individual cases may however be illuminating to the remedial teacher. The important point is that a minimum level of oral competence is necessary for reading to have any point at all.

The development of oral competence is an important area of teaching in its own right. Some formal assessment of oracy as an independent language skill is possible — particularly in the form of listening skill. Traditionally listening tests have really been based on comprehension of orally presented prose. Recently, however, group tests of comprehension of real spoken language have been produced (Wilkinson, Stratta and Dudley, 1974).

These *Listening Comprehension Tests* consist of three batteries suited respectively to ten- to eleven-year-olds, thirteen- to fourteen-year-olds and seventeen- to eighteen-year-olds. The test materials are tape recordings and are used to assess a number of listening skills. As well as fairly straightforward tests of understanding and inference from context, tests are included which deal with understanding of the meanings implied by the stresses and emphases of speech, knowledge of register and ability to appreciate the human relationships implied in speech. The materials are all examples of real spoken language, rather than orally-delivered written prose.

There is no easy answer to the assessment of speaking ability however. Some assessment of the technical maturity of speech is possible only given time and resources beyond many schools. The

Speaking sections of the NFER tests do provide means of assessment along these lines for the more enterprising teacher. Speaking ability however has much more to it than this, and is essentially a matter of being able to produce language which is appropriate to each real life situation the speaker finds himself in. It is the great flexibility of skill required which makes formal assessment impractical. Teachers could however make greater use of a less objective procedure such as a check-list of oral skills.

Spelling

Pupils with reading problems are likely to have spelling problems also, although there are fluent readers who are nevertheless poor spellers and only a few standardized tests of spelling are available. Schonell's *Graded Word Spelling Test* and sub-test II of the *Standard Reading Tests* are the most widely used and both have norms which are probably now out of date — spelling standards may have risen or fallen since they were produced. A number of more recently normed tests include spelling as part of a general assessment of English, for example the NFER *English Progress Tests* the *Richmond Tests of Basic Skills* and the *Bristol Achievement Tests: English Language*.

There has been little research into the validity of any of the ways these tests measure spelling achievement. In particular the relationship between test performance and the extent to which children actually spell competently in everyday written work in schools has not been examined — although this would seem to be a crucial question. Many teachers will have experience of pupils who do not habitually spell well, but who can maintain an extra degree of care and accuracy for the duration of a formal test in which they know spelling 'matters today'.

Margaret Peters (1967) has suggested that assessment of attainment is less important than assessment of basic spelling ability and diagnosis of particular spelling problems. The tests used in the *SRA Spelling Laboratory 11a* and the *Schonell Diagnostic Spelling Tests* are both diagnostic in function, although their approach is different. The Schonell tests examine basic difficulties in spelling, while the SRA test surveys knowledge of a large number of spelling rules and one or two persistent areas of difficulty such as the spelling of homophones. With the exception of these two there do not appear to be any very scientific or systematic methods of assessing spelling. One alternative for the enterprising would be to use the dictation tests which were used for research by Margaret Peters and which can be found in the appendices of her book *Success in Spelling* (1970).

Frankly, none of the tests available at present seem to be very satisfactory. The attainment tests tend to treat spelling attainment as a simple analogue to reading ability — a matter of being able to spell (as opposed to read) increasingly hard words. A fairer measure of spelling attainment might be obtained by simply counting the number of mis-spellings in a random sample of the pupil's own writing. It would not be impossible for norms to be produced for this kind of assessment, although as yet none have been produced. This approach concentrates not so much on which 'hard words' a pupil can spell, but on how good a speller he is in relation to what he actually writes.

This distinction between 'good' and 'poor' spellers — regardless of age — is the one that Margaret Peters suggests is most suitable for assessment of the skill. She suggests criteria for the identification of good and poor spellers which range from effectiveness of visual imagery and letter-memory-span to the pupil's concept of himself as a good or poor speller. Again, these ideas could probably be converted into an objective test, but regrettably no such instrument has yet been developed.

English attainment

A distinction is made by test publishers between tests of Reading and tests of English or English Language. This distinction is useful for many practical purposes, but it would be hard to prove that there are two separate abilities called Reading and English. In fact, the two most widely used series of English tests, the *NFER English Progress Tests* and the *Bristol Achievement Series Tests of English Language*, both involve a substantial amount of reading work. Their claim to be English rather than Reading tests is based on the inclusion of some items dealing with spelling, organization of ideas, and possibly some structured writing tasks. These latter questions are however a far cry from real continuous writing work — surely the essence of much English teaching, regardless of how 'progressive' or 'traditional' the teacher.

Validity of English tests

The aims and values of English teachers often range wider than the content of standardized tests to include literature, drama and thematic work. English tests cannot be expected to predict exactly how pupils will cope with work in such areas. On the other hand it may well be the case that until a pupil has reached a minimum threshold of success in the basics he will enjoy little success in an English course, however much the teacher attempts to obviate the difficulties and stimulate interest. It is for reasons such as this that the assessment of reading in the remedial context needs to consider the pupil's relative standing in formal basic writing skills.

The English test tends to break down English into component skills. This may not be made explicit by the test constructor but it is usually easy to see what distinctions are implied by different test tasks. This raises problems very similar to those encountered with sub-skills of reading. The reader may recall that while a multifacet approach to testing might be thought to be desirable, it did not follow that sub-skills and part-scores could necessarily be treated as statistically separate. English attainment involves much material which can be formally taught at the level of knowledge and application of rules, so that a group of pupils might show they had been well drilled in punctuation but be less adept at putting scrambled sentences in sequence to form a paragraph. However the underlying ability is probably not sectioned in this manner. Test standardization samples rarely exhibit such differences with sufficient uniformity for such distinctions to be made by the test constructor on empirical grounds.

The English attainment test is perhaps best employed as an adjunct to the reading test as it gives a second estimate of a pupil's literacy by testing some communicative skills, albeit indirectly and in somewhat artificial situations. The use of two test scores will also reduce the likelihood of error in assessment of the individual pupils, and it is sometimes easier or more acceptable to speak of a pupil as 'weak at English' rather than 'backward in reading'. However the English test itself is often more time-consuming to mark than a reading test and the weak reader may find the test more daunting to complete: it lends itself less well to grading of tasks from easy to difficult and the instructions for items often constitute a reading comprehension task in their own right!

Writing ability

We can thus regard English tests as primarily reading tests with some additional coverage of writing skills. Such tests are however far from adequate in this respect in view of the great importance of writing skill. In practice most teachers keep a running assessment of pupils' writing ability simply by setting writing work, and marking it. This is however a highly subjective and informal kind of assessment, and just occasionally something more formal might be needed. In practice there are very few really sound methods available and the remarks which follow deal with the theoretical possibilities.

In the US more direct objective tests of writing ability have been evolved. These include the interlinear task in which a poorly written passage with a given number of errors has to be corrected by the pupil. A variation on this theme is an entirely mechanical multiple-choice format in which the pupil endorses certain possible corrections, amendments and critical comments about a test passage with deliberate errors in it. Such techniques are highly objective and reliable and have been statistically validated. Their mechanistic treatment of writing has been criticized however, and they appear to be more tests of editorial skill than communication. In any case no such tests are at present available to UK teachers.

For some time 'readability' formulae have been used to determine the reading age for which books are suitable. It would be possible to give an essay a reading level age, thus estimate a writing age for the pupil. Such a technique might be useful for assessment at a remedial level, where it could be treated as a desirable dimension of sophistication. Ultimately, however readability is concerned with incomprehensibility of prose. Its use might not be positively related to efforts to teach clear and effective written composition once the readability of pupils' prose reaches a certain point of development.

It may eventually prove possible to assess some of the mechanical aspects of writing ability by linguistic analysis. Hunt (1968), for example, experimented with the technique of presenting pupils of different ages with a prose passage written in extremely short sentences. The passage was extremely abrupt and choppy and pupils were instructed to re-write it in more acceptable English, but without omitting any of the factual content. Various linguistic analyses were applied to the pupils' versions in an attempt to find effective measures of syntactic maturity, notably the T-unit, which is essentially a main clause and any related subordinate clauses. The results were based on too small a sample to provide normative data, but it did appear that measures such as mean T-unit length were a fair index of the development of syntax.

Berse (1974) experimented with a range of linguistic criteria for the assessment of children's free-writing. The results of the experiment suggested that measures such as pre-verb length, counts of vocabulary and use of modifying clauses might be useful criteria for evaluating composition.

Such work is however largely experimental. Little is yet known about the reliability and objectivity of such schemes of analysis, the ease with which they can be applied by teachers or the normative values to be attached to them.

Their use is in any case likely to be largely restricted to the assessment of the early development of writing skill and remedial work. Syntax is only a single aspect of writing skill, even in its simple everyday uses.

Although it is difficult to make any kind of in-depth assessment of samples of written work a general assessment can be made with much more confidence. The effectiveness of multiple-marking of essays by teams of appraisal markers has been well established — see *Schools Council Examinations Bulletin No.12: Multiple Marking of English Compositions*. This technique however would seem to be mainly relevant in the context of examinations and large-scale assessment, rather than as techniques closely geared to teaching.

It would be pointless to pretend that the assessment techniques described in this chapter really do English and language teaching justice. The limitations of the techniques stem partly from the complex nature of language itself and from the English teacher's concern with cultural values and individual responses which are not testable. It would be foolish to belittle such objections, but at the same time some of the inadequacy of tests stems from the unwillingness of many teachers to really become involved in development of better techniques and the ignorance of test constructors about the nature of language and values of English teaching. These are problems which may eventually be resolved so that more effective assessment materials become available.

Chapter Eight

Diagnostic testing

Much has now been said about what seems to be only a preliminary — the identification of children with reading problems from a larger group. Certainly many teachers when asked about their testing requirements emphasize the need for tests of some kind to help diagnose the problems of individual readers. In contrast, they may express impatience with the limitations of group attainment tests. If one is new to the business of teaching reading, particularly in a remedial context, one may be at a loss how to set about sizing-up pupils. It is in such circumstances that the teacher may well wonder whether a test of some kind might help, by enabling him to make the same kind of clinical diagnosis that the expert would make. Sadly it must be admitted from the start that the contribution of tests in diagnosis is much more restricted than is often assumed. To rely largely on published tests is not likely to solve one's diagnostic problems once and for all. At best, they are a starting point.

The hypothetical expert would probably make his diagnosis in an *ad hoc* manner using any one of a number of tasks at his disposal, depending upon his feelings for the situation, prior knowledge of the pupil, or the outcome of informally chatting to him. If it suits his style of teaching some kind of published individual testing procedure may be included in the process, but this is by no means a universal practice. Kohl (1974) contrasts the elaborate battery of diagnostic tests used by the more technically-minded reading clinics with his own far less dramatic request to the pupil to read a passage from a book. From this he can make the kinds of observations which in his experience have proved useful. In simple terms, diagnosis consists in asking the learner to attempt certain tasks and forming insights about his difficulties by observing his performance. Selection of the appropriate tasks and interpreting the results are a matter of skill rather than science.

The problem is that this kind of skill comes only with experience and many people will be very much less sure of what particular tasks to set, or questions to ask. For them a reasonable alternative way of starting to teach a reader with difficulties would be to make use of existing structures and materials that will 'point them in the right direction' and give them some confidence. The teacher who sets out in this way may later turn to more flexible approaches such as the *Informal Reading Inventory* (described in Chapter Four) or to some even more personal and *ad hoc* approach.

Occasionally he may remain content to work within the structure of a published test. This is often a quite justifiable strategy, but the adherent must be sure in his own mind that there is no question of 'hiding behind the test', i.e. that the test is actively a help in coming to grips with the reader's difficulties rather than putting off the need to do so.

The would-be user of diagnostic tests should bear in mind that in any case no reading specialist, clinic or centre would rely solely on the findings of a formal diagnostic test. Even where these are used they are accompanied by a great deal of extra observation made in the course of administering the test and in further informal probing. The tests will not be treated in a literal-minded way. Although the testing procedures should be strictly followed — particularly if any form of score is to be obtained and recorded — this does not preclude the tester from drawing all kinds of incidental inferences. Very often these will have the most significance for subsequent teaching. It should also not be overlooked that many of the most simple attainment tests, such as the Graded Word Reading tests are used in this way. Challenge any experienced teacher as to why he uses a seemingly antiquated or simple test of this kind. It is quite likely he will reply that the score he gets at the end is of little importance. He uses the test as it provides an opportunity for the formation of both a general impression of the reader and of his particular difficulties. A diagnostic test will probably lend itself to this approach more fully, but a teacher will use whatever materials are to hand. In fact there is no ultimate reason why any published tests must be used in this way, in preference to material of the teacher's own choice and devising.

It is thus not necessary to use published diagnostic tests in order to be a good diagnostician. Tests generally only supply a structure which the less experienced can follow with some confidence, but which the individual teacher may outgrow in time. The best diagnostic testing device is quite simply an experienced and skilled teacher in reading. In the absence of such a device there is no shame in using a test, but the newcomer to teaching reading should not assume that the best diagnosing is done in this way. The following section will discuss why this should be so.

'Diagnosis': its limits in test-form

So far in this chapter it has been established that it is by no means the sign of an expert to use a diagnostic test, but such a test can provide a useful initial structure for diagnosis. If tests are to be used effectively at all, it is crucial their limitations are considered first. This section will discuss why such tests are intrinsically limited. However it must be stressed that the reservations expressed are not intended destructively, but merely to quicken the test user's awareness of the possibilities and limitations of his materials.

In the first place, a diagnostic test will probably not explain *why* a reader is failing. It will not, in a word, point to the ultimate cause of the difficulty. To find out why this should be so one could turn to the published literature on reading failure. It will soon become apparent that there is great variation in the types of difficulties and their causes. No one test could ever hope to cover all of them — probably many of them are untestable anyway.

A more convenient and rapid way of getting a similar answer might be to talk with a remedial teacher, or even to pause for reflection upon cases of children one has taught or is teaching. In either case it will probably emerge that the causes or likely causes of their difficulty are varied and many. In some cases a number of factors — again untestable ones — will be working together. In other cases poor reading may be a symptom of wider social or personal difficulties. In others there may be no cause; it may just be the case that the child is already reading as well as he can in view of his limited capabilities (the identification of slow learners as opposed to underachievers has already been mentioned). Certainly the teacher of reading may have to work — at least within the classroom — on the symptoms of reading difficulty rather than their supposed causes. It is in fact rarely fruitful to make an analogy between reading difficulty and 'disease'. Although one may detect some kind of cause for reading failure by examining a pupil's long-term case history it is unlikely that any 'antibiotic' can be administered. Certainly it is unlikely that the test will provide the 'microscope' with which a 'reading virus' will be detected.

A similar kind of analogy might be drawn between reading and a specific fault in a machine. This sometimes seems a fairer analogy. Just as a machine may not function properly because of a defective component so a reader may not read properly because of some specific disability. Here, surely a test instrument of some kind would be appropriate? Yet while there is some substance to this view, there is great danger in using the analogy too freely or widely. While it is always possible to be explicit about what it is a reader cannot do, it does not follow that these are the exact reasons *why* he cannot read. Specific difficulties such as confusion of 'b', 'd' and 'p', or inability to

discriminate between vowel sounds or to make use of context when reading, may be symptoms rather than real causes. The test may draw the teacher's attention to the presence of these problems, but it will be up to him to interpret their significance.

We should also remember that the 'cause' which has prevented a child from succeeding *so far* may not be a permanent obstacle. For example, a child whose failure is attributed to social deprivation may, in a new situation, begin to learn to read, while remaining socially deprived. Here the cause remains, but its effects and symptoms are shown to be remediable. Thus, while this teacher should always endeavour to find out why a child is having difficulty (if possible), this should be done so that appropriate teaching can be given. Removal of the cause may be a valid long-term aspiration, but this may not be an absolute necessity before one can hope to teach the child.

A diagnostic type of test thus provides at best a more detailed mapping-out of the immediate problem. Just as the attainment test attempts to describe the 'state of reading' within a group, so the diagnostic test will describe it within an individual. The operative word here is description as opposed to explanation. It may well be that the test will direct the teacher towards an explanation of his own, but the test itself cannot provide it. Reading difficulty does not lend itself to miraculous or magical solutions, and the teacher who is dismayed by the complexity of the problems he is faced with should not then expect too much of a mere test.

The rationale of diagnostic testing

Diagnostic tests — the term is rather a loose one — are thus really an extension of the mapping process which can be started with attainment tests. The reader will be relieved to learn that the technical and statistical aspect of testing is generally far less important in most kinds of diagnostic testing. The diagnostic approach is usually concerned with the individual in his own right and not with comparing him statistically with others. In diagnostic testing it is more important that the right questions and tasks are set. If the testing is to lead fairly directly to teaching — the main reason for the exercise in the first place — it is crucial that the content of the test is meaningfully related to the skills which are to be taught. There are two ways in which this can be done, and they reflect two different meanings of the loose term 'diagnosis'.

Diagnosis through attainment profiles

This approach has already been introduced in the chapter dealing with profiles of attainment in different skill areas and the use of sub-test scores. It is re-introduced here partly because all of the reservations mentioned above about what we mean by diagnosis and what we should expect from diagnostic tests apply to such an approach.

A more important reason for raising the issue again is to make more explicit the way in which such an approach if developed fully, can work diagnostically. In Chapter Four we were concerned with showing how the 'multifaceted' approach to testing could be handled so that a cross-section of tests could be assembled to give a fair representation of the various aspects of reading attainment that the teacher wished to measure. This is a diagnostic principle which can be applied individually.

When the teacher gets down to individual cases this approach can have useful implications for individual teaching. For example, a pupil's profile may show a quite distinct 'low' in one particular area. The scores for the pupil in Figure 8A show that he is a mediocre performer on tests of silent reading (vocabulary and comprehension) and that he is of average ability in verbal reasoning and distinctly above average in non-verbal reasoning and mathematics. His very low score in the test of reading rate provides a clue to the difficulty. The teacher interpreting the profile may justly wonder whether exercises designed to give more pace to his reading would result in improvements in reading attainment and verbal reasoning test performance. The problem may simply be one of slowness.

The pupil in Figure 8B is average for his age in oral word-recognition, but his performance on a silent sentence-completion test suggests he has failed to extend simple comprehension skills and that his knowledge of meaning is less satisfactory. On this evidence the teacher might consider work which concentrated upon vocabulary and sentence-structure.

These examples could however be misleading. In many cases easily-interpretable discrepancies of this kind may not appear. As has been pointed out, reading test scores tend to be highly correlated with each other. Further, the results lead only to generalizations about appropriate teaching. It is left to the teacher to decide what exercises and methods should be employed.

Which tests should be included in a profile?

For assessment of 'reading readiness' this question is answered by the test constructor who normally produces reading readiness tests as a complete battery or set of profiles. The materials included usually cover important areas such as visual and auditory perception, linguistic development and mental maturity, through a comprehensive series of sub-tests. Outside this area there are few tests which come in ready-made sets in this way. Most publishers will endeavour to ensure a basic degree of comparability between tests in their overall range, so that tests of English, Mathematics and Study Skills can be compared

Figure 8A: Profile for six test scores

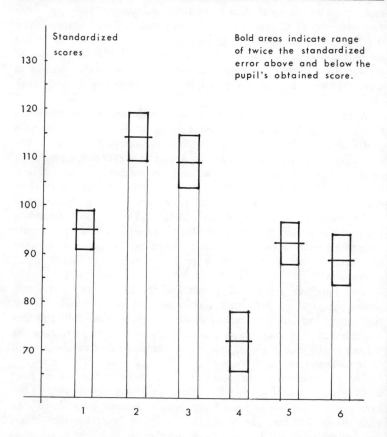

Test	Standard Error for Test	Pupil's Standardized Score	Range in which 'True' Score lies
1. Verbal Reasoning	2.0	95	91–99
2. Non-Verbal Reasoning	2.5	114	109–119
3. Mathematics	2.7	109	103.6–114.4
4. Reading Rate	3.0	72	66–78
5. Reading Vocabulary	2.1	92	87.8–96.2
6. Reading Comprehension	2.7	89	83.6–94.4

Figure 8B: Profile comparing chronological age and reading age (oral and silent)

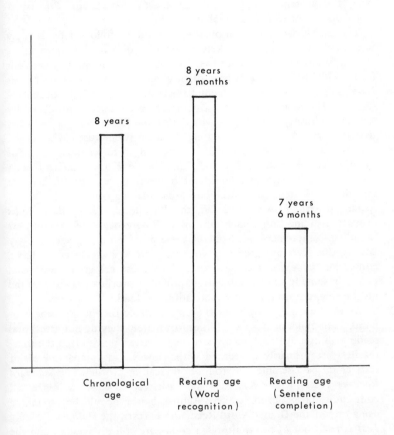

directly, as in the *Bristol Series of Achievement Tests.* This arrangement is however a rather general one.

A more detailed diagnostic battery will have to be assembled on an *ad hoc* basis. The final selection will depend very much on what is already known about the child or children to be assessed and the kinds of skills to be taught.

Where the children to be assessed are likely to have a range of problems and the need is for comprehensive coverage some general suggestions can be made. In the first instance a simple and easy test of word-recognition should be included. If a reading age scale is to be used throughout the *Southgate Group Reading Test 1* might make a suitable start. For a standardized score scale the *Gates-McGinitie Primary A Vocabulary Test* would be suitable.

The simple word-recognition stage should be followed by an easy test which uses a test-task likely to involve some of the intermediate reading skills, and a sentence-based test provides the most convenient form. Both the above tests have slightly more advanced versions of this type associated with them. Beyond this a more demanding vocabulary test is likely to be useful and a comprehensive range is produced by various publishers. Young's *Group Reading Test* and the NFER's *Reading Tests A* and *BD* are among the most widely used at this level. Tests of this kind can extend in application up to secondary age, for example, *NFER Reading Test EH-1* and the *Widespan Reading Test*. A really comprehensive profile should however go a stage further and include an element of continuous prose reading, such as the *NFER Reading Comprehension Test DE*, the *Richmond Test of Basic Skills* (Test R, Reading Comprehension) or the *Progressive Achievement Test* (Reading Comprehension). None of these provide reading ages directly and at this level only the *Gap Reading Test* — a cloze test — has a conversion table for reading ages. All of these are group tests, and could, in some form of combination, provide a profile of skills from the most elementary to those of a more advanced kind.

As they are all group tests they are suitable for the assessment of numbers of children at a time, but unfortunately they do not assess oral reading ability, although in the remedial context this is often the thing teachers are primarily concerned with. However, a comparable set of tests could be assembled to produce oral reading profiles. The *Standard Reading Tests* include very easy and basic tests at word, sentence and continuous prose levels, while a similar battery could be assembled using one of the Graded Word Recognition Tests, the *Holborn Reading Test* (this is out of print, although copies are still obtainable) and the Neale *Analysis of Reading Ability*. Indeed, there is a good case for using both oral and silent reading tests in a diagnostic profile.

The tests described above are not recommended as a universal group, likely to produce meaningful profiles for any child. Many of them would be suitable for a child who has reached the level of skill of an average seven-year-old, and some would be suited to readers somewhat below this level. The difficulty is that a child's chronological age is no guide to suitable tests if he has difficulty in reading. A crucial element of judgement thus remains.

The profile approach to diagnosis has the advantage that it can be conducted through group testing and that there is a wide range of

Figure 8C: Profile comparing chronological age with a variety of Reading Age test scores.

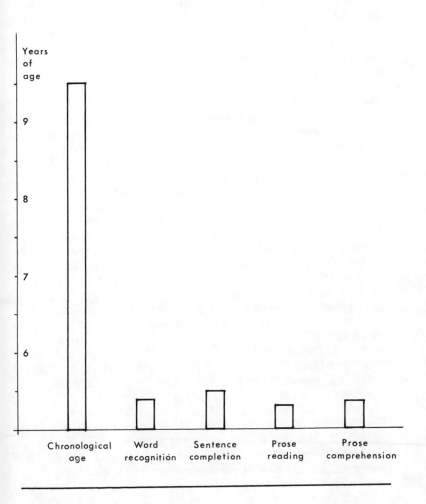

published tests which could be included. There are however practical disadvantages due to cost and marking time, and it must be remembered that where there is no discrepancy (i.e. in many cases) the exercises will have been of little use. The point is made in the extreme case of the pupil in Figure 8C. Here an array of tests have been given, and time has been spent in administration and marking, yet little has been learned about the pupil — except possibly about his resistance to stress in view of the number of tests involved! The reader may care to pause to consider what other conclusion one can draw from the profile before continuing with the next section.

Further diagnosis

It did not require tests to establish that the pupil in Table 8C was virtually a non-reader! This does however bring out a final problem with the attainment profile. It does not have much application where reading is very poor indeed and the pupil has not yet mastered the initial decoding and word-recognition skills. There is a need for a much more fundamental kind of examination before teaching can commence.

Consider also the profile in Figure 8D. Here the pupil has a moderate oral vocabulary, as indicated by the *English Picture Vocabulary Test*. He has a rudimentary sight vocabulary — he knows the objects to which a few of the printed words in the Gates-McGinitie Test refer. However, he seems to have made little progress in phonic and decoding skills. His score on the Carver *Word Recognition Test* is less than could be gained by guessing. His chronological age can be taken to show that he has passed the age at which reading is initially taught. Accordingly some quite thorough investigation is required which lies beyond the scope of group testing.

This profile was hypothetical; however, in the case of a real child all kinds of additional questions would be asked about the medical and social background at the outset. Quite possibly referral to an educational psychologist would be in order.

Mention of the educational psychologist brings us to a major consideration in individual testing. Where there is clearly a need for individually testing a child in-depth, highly specialized tests are available. These might be used if it is suspected that the child is of very low intelligence — possibly needing education in a special school — or where specific psychological functions are impaired. These could indicate the need for specialized attention. Testing to firmly establish this often involves tests which require the tester to have the appropriate special training in the use of the test. In Britain it is rare for teachers to have such training and almost invariably such work is done by educational psychologists. Again, the test may then only be regarded as a useful or incidental sort of guide — not on its own as any

Figure 8D: Profile of a backward reader

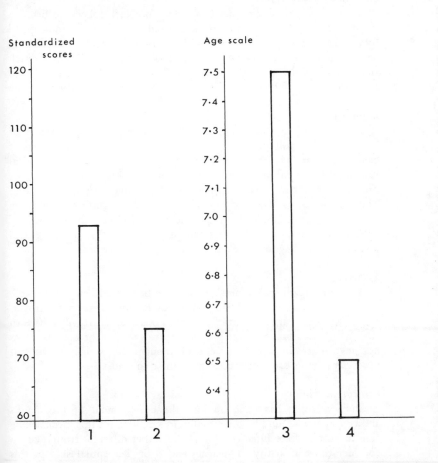

Key: 1 English Picture Vocabulary Test
        2 Gates McGinitie Primary A (Vocabulary)
        3 Chronological Age
        4 Carver Word Recognition Test

form of absolute proof. Such tests are thus by no means indispensable and when used they will be backed-up by all kinds of incidental and additional observations.

The teacher of reading need not therefore feel obliged to become highly informed about the more specialized tests, or feel handicapped by not having the specialist training. Their use is confined to a relatively small number of children with exceptional difficulties. There is much that can be done with the materials that are available to teachers. Moreover the purely clinical test is not concerned directly with the business of teaching reading — though properly interpreted it may have implications.

For the teacher who wishes to go beyond the profile-based form of diagnosis, while still relying upon published materials, two main lines of examination are available. The first is to look at forms of psychological functioning which are related to reading and are some form of prerequisites for it — such as perceptual and linguistic development. The second is to examine the child's word-recognition skills in a systematic form, through a phonic test. Indeed, these lines of investigation may well be dictated as a result of a more general profile-form of diagnosis such as that previously described.

1. Pre-reading

The term 'reading readiness' might have been used here just as well. However the term has confusing implications, some of them controversial. It will be returned to briefly later in this chapter. It will suffice to say here that certain tests are pre-reading tests in that the test task does not involve reading, but some skill thought to be helpful (if not necessary) for subsequent success in learning to read.

Perceptual skills

Much research has gone on into the development of the child's ability to *perceive* aurally and visually. In simple terms this means being able to hear and see *intelligently*. This is rather different from medical considerations of acuity of hearing and sight. Perceptual skill in this sense concerns the meaning and use which the child can make of raw sound and sight impressions.

In the first instance it is of course necessary to be quite certain a pupil's sight and hearing are satisfactory so these can be ruled out as causes of difficulty. A teacher can informally test a child's vision and hearing and should be alert to the possibility of undetected defects. However thorough testing in this area is really the concern of school medical services. Medical screening will leave the possibility of perceptual difficulties unexamined. In test task terms this is usually a matter of testing the child's capacity to detect differences (discrimination) between similar sounds or between similar shapes or letters.

The teacher who is new to the teaching of reading should perhaps pause to reflect on why these two skills are so important. Hopefully it will become clear that inability to tell the difference between sounds and shapes would make it hard to effectively turn printed words into their corresponding spoken form. A child to whom many letter shapes 'look the same' or sound the same will clearly have difficulty learning to read.

The standard test task for auditory discrimination requires the tester to dictate pairs of words which sound similar, together with pairs made up of the same word,

e.g.   'tell — tail'
             'run — run' etc.

The testee has to say whether each pair is the 'same' or 'different'. Published tests, such as Wepman's *Auditory Discrimination Test* or Test P5 of the *Domain Phonic Tests* are so devised as to give a systematic coverage of sounds.

Visual tests are more varied in form, but in general they range from the perception of fairly crude differences in diagrams and pictures, to various inversions, reversals and distortions of print.

Of equal importance to discrimination skills are those of sequencing — the ability to remember sequences of sounds or symbols. In test terms this usually involves the presentation of a series of sounds, words, pictures or symbols to the child. The child then has to reproduce these from memory.

Again, some reflection might be worthwhile — why should memory for sequences be important? The answer is — in brief — that to reproduce a word effectively the pupil must not only recognize the difference between letter symbols but hold them in his memory long enough to blend and reproduce them as a word. Beyond this, whole words must be remembered as meaningful sentences.

Thus the more thorough diagnostic tests — for example the *Aston Index* includes tasks of sequencing. Beyond this type of testing the teacher has the choice of much more informal tasks of his own devising, possibly along the lines of the 'Form Perception Test' described by Tansley (1967).

Satisfactory perceptual development is crucial for success at reading but in many circumstances it may well be unnecessary to feel obliged to obtain and employ a formal published test. If visual and auditory perception are a problem this should rapidly become apparent in the course of attempting to teach. A test of the teacher's own devising might be used to confirm the teacher's suspicions and to alert him to the nature of this problem.

If the tests of visual perception do happen to bring to light really severe perceptual difficulty a more thorough examination using a test such as the Frostig *Test of Perceptual Development* (see Chapter Twelve) might be used, but analysis beyond this stage is definitely the province of the specialist. Hopefully for most children any initial basic diagnosis of perception will lead to teaching rather than further test-probing.

Motor skills

A thorough investigation of a child's reading difficulties might well involve tests of physical skills and development. As with so many aspects of diagnosis an informal approach would satisfy many teachers. Sullivan and Humphrey (1973) describe very fully how simple physical activities and tasks can be used by teachers in both assessment and teaching of reading. However commercially produced test-materials often include standard procedures for the appraisal of motor difficulties. These range from simple copying tasks, involving either abstract figures or printed words to more complex maze tracing and line joining. The former are exemplified by sub-tests in Daniels' and Diack's *Standard Reading Tests*, the latter by sub-tests of the Frostig *Test of Visual Perception*. The emphasis in most such test tasks is not upon coordination of physical movement with other skills — particularly visual-perception. It is in this area of motor skill coordination that some very important observations can be made by the teacher informally and incidentally without recourse to specially produced materials. Co-ordination and control of eye movement can, for example, be observed with special cameras; however, an adequate do-it-yourself procedure is described by Ruth Strang in the *Diagnostic Teaching of Reading* (Chapter Nine) with no more hardware than a piece of card with a hole in it.

Similarly the child's ability to detect and reproduce rhythm *could* be tested with elaborate pre-recorded exercises but an informal 'tapping test' in which the child has to repeat a sequence tapped-out by the teacher is quite adequate.

Difficulty in learning to read is thought sometimes to be due particularly to the child's failure to develop lateral dominance — i.e. left or right 'handedness' and 'footedness' associated with the growth of dominance in one of the hemispheres of the brain. The *Harris Test of Lateral Dominance* provides a standard procedure and materials for assessing this. Again simple exercises devised by the teacher could be used equally well. Stephen Jackson in *Get Reading Right* (1971) exemplifies some simple training exercises which could equally be used diagnostically.

Mental ability

An investigation of a child's thinking (cognitive) skills and mental ability normally figure in a diagnostic approach. This may be confined to a simple general appraisal of the child's general mental capacities along the group test lines described in previous chapters. Alternatively an individual test of intelligence such as the *Stanford-Binet* may be given by a psychologist. This is normally used to ascertain whether poor progress in reading is in fact a reflection of the child's overall mental limitations. The psychologist may however use the testing-situation to make extra and incidental observations. These in turn may prove more informative than a bland record of the 'official' test results. In cases of very severe difficulty a qualitative picture may be sought using tests such as the *Illinois Test of Psycholinguistic Abilities* (ITPA) (Kirk *et al.*, 1968). Here the aim is to pick out and isolate highly specific areas of cognitive difficulty. This concern with relating reading difficulty to specific cognitive processes and functions is rather different from the application of a 'blanket' mental test. This approach may one day prove useful, but in the present state many of the test techniques are largely experimental. Elaborate tests of this kind are rarely available for use by teachers. In fact the usefulness of such tests for the appraisal of the majority of children is probably slight. Newcomer and Hammill (1975) reviewed a large number of experimental studies involving the ITPA and concluded that its validity as either a predictor of school success or as a diagnostic instrument was far from proven.

A teacher wishing to use cognitive tests in the probing of reading difficulty might find a study of some of the research reports on reading difficulty useful. A convenient collection of such studies can be found in Jessie Reid's *Reading: Problems and Practices* (1972). It would however be very misleading to suggest that an immersion in such an approach would make one a dramatically more effective teacher of reading.

Linguistic ability

Reading is a skill which involves obtaining meaning from language. Initially the reader is taught to break the 'code' which is used to store language on the printed page. However no one would call the sheer process of learning the sounds associated with print 'reading'. The reader has to understand the sense conveyed by the language. It follows that if his own ability to use and understand spoken language is limited he will make little progress with printed and written forms. A major consideration for the diagnostician must therefore be the reader's existing linguistic skill. As in other areas much will be done informally — the teacher will form an impression of the extent of the child's vocabulary and his understanding and use of structures and expressions in the spoken medium.

Assessment of language is however a delicate process and the impression formed by the teacher will be very prone to distortions brought about by the subjectivity of the individual examiner.

Assessment will be coloured by the teacher's own linguistic background. The whole matter of language, class and education is the subject of much dispute in which ideology and research findings are confused. Accordingly, although we may be sure that the tests available probably represent an oversimplification of the nature of language skill, there is some case for the use of such techniques to act as an anchor and reference point.

At a simple level it is possible to assess knowledge of word-meanings using the *English Picture Vocabulary Test*. Here the testee has to find the pictured object or activity which goes with the word dictated by the tester. Three forms of this test exist for individual testing at the pre-school age to group tests for secondary and adult testees. Mastery of language is however much more than just knowledge of individual word-meanings. In real life the child has to communicate and receive meaning in continuous form.

Tests for comprehension of continuous samples of spoken material have existed in the US for some time. Recently, listening comprehension tests have been developed in the UK, for example the NFER publishes *Tests of Proficiency in English* which include tests of both speaking and listening ability. These tests are at three levels, dealing respectively with single word meaning, sentences, and continuous prose.

Although initially intended for non-native speakers of English, these tests are generally useful for assessment of language difficulty in the first two years of schooling. By combining with tests of reading and writing, and providing common material across modes, the tests can be used to assess the degree of discrepancy which may exist between any two modes. For example, a child may understand more than he can say or write, or poor listening comprehension may emerge as a possible source of difficulty in other modes of communication.

Here a need for caution must be indicated. Although success in reading relies on satisfactory competence in spoken language, the glib assumptions which can follow from this must be avoided. In particular, spoken language is not identical to written language. Thus competence in spoken modes cannot be a perfect reflection of understanding of written language. American tests of listening comprehension characteristically use a 'talking book' format and have made no attempt to use real spoken language. Instead the test material is written prose, orally presented. This gives the test greater face validity as an indicator of potential for comprehension of printed language. The research on the subject partly supports this view. Listening and reading comprehension tend to be related. However the evidence is not unequivocal. Not all experimental studies have found listening to be strong indicators of reading potential. A particularly sophisticated study by Milton L. Clarke (1973) found listening ability and reading to be relatively distinct from each other. This would cast some doubt on the likelihood of a simple relationship between reading and listening. The best construction to put on this situation is probably that while we cannot make any categorical interpretation of the results of an oral type of test, they may be usefully suggestive. In the first place they may be set aside the subjective appraisals of the teacher. They may thus be used to help show the need for more pre-reading work and for general language enrichment. They may less readily be taken as indicators of reading potential. To put it another way, the orally 'bright' pupil who understands little orally will probably have similar − if not greater − difficulties in reading.

Reading readiness

As has been noted, satisfactory development of perceptual skills is thought to be a precondition for successful reading progress. Thus many tests which place emphasis upon perception could be regarded as reading-readiness tests. They deal with skills which are a precondition for success in learning to read. Tests such as the *Frostig Test of Perceptual Development* and the *Standard Reading Tests* are effectually tests of reading-readiness although not explicitly designated as such by their publishers. Similarly the areas typically covered by most reading-readiness tests − visual and auditory discrimination, motor control and coordination, general mental ability and vocabulary − are just the areas in which basic diagnosis is applied.

In addition both kinds of tests deal similarly with cognitive processes such as the capacity to relate pictures, sounds and words to their written symbols; memory span and letter recognition may be tested. Sequencing tasks are often employed in this context, whereby the child has to recall or re-create a given visual or auditory sequence.

Some prominence may also be given to phonic readiness in the form of tests of sound blending. Published tests such as the *Standard Reading Tests* and the *Neale Analysis of Reading Ability* include basic blending tasks, although as with many diagnostic tasks teachers could fairly easily devise their own. Most reading-readiness tests are of US construction and their norms refer to US samples. It is sometimes suggested that such tests can be regarded as criterion-referenced so that a British child who was 'unready' by US norm-standards would probably be unable to learn to read in the British situation.

However the validity of testing for readiness is by no means fully established or accepted. Pupils may learn to read without reaching the test criteria of readiness, while others who have reached the criterial level may not make much initial progress. This perhaps reflects the weakness of the reading readiness concept, rather than faults in the content of the tests.

The validity of most such tests is predictive — they provide an indication of likely later success or failure at reading. Rarely is it demonstrated that the tests can be used to *avoid* failure in practice. This however is the way they should be used by the teacher, i.e. to indicate what further experience activities (pre-reading or otherwise) could fruitfully be next used.

The whole concept of reading-readiness is well explained in Downing and Thackray's *Reading-Readiness* (1971). The teacher who wishes to make use of formal testing would be well advised to consult such a text in order to be clear in her own mind what is meant by the idea. Above all, the misconception that tests can be used as an exam for 'entrance' into a reading instruction course should be discarded.

Basic-type profiles

There is no reason why the basics of perception, language, motor skills and cognitive functioning should not be compared in profiles. Indeed there is every advantage in analysing them along similar lines to attainment profiles. Unfortunately tests of these skills often fail to have a common scale — an essential for any kind of comparative profile. Tests which are presented as a self-contained battery are thus at an advantage here, as a common scale can be built in with ease. This may vary from a simple form point profile such as that of the *Thackray Reading-Readiness Profiles* to the more sophisticated percentile-based profiles of the *Harrison-Stroud Reading-Readiness Profiles*.

By far the most developed area of reading diagnosis is that of word analysis and phonic knowledge and skill. This kind of testing is basic in that phonic decoding — the getting of word sounds from printed letter symbols — is fundamental in learning to read in the initial stages. At the same time diagnostic phonic testing is well within the scope of the average teacher. Indeed a number of very thorough and comprehensive published tests are available.

The basic technique is to have the pupil read aloud a passage or series of words so that weaknesses in word-attack, blending and sound-knowledge can be identified and recorded. This covers two levels of diagnosis: oral reading of continuous prose, as required in the *Neale Analysis of Reading Ability* and the *Durell Analysis of Reading Difficulty*, will reveal general weakness in a pupils' strategy such as a reluctance to attempt unfamiliar words or a tendency to omit, reverse and substitute particular elements. More recently, Marie Clay (1972b) has suggested a revised scheme for analysis of errors on the Neale test —

or indeed any informal test of oral prose reading.

At a more detailed level individual words may be presented for oral reading as in the *Domain Test of Phonic Skills*, so that problems of blending, syllabication and recognition of individual letter sounds, blends and diagraphs may be tested. The words are chosen to reflect particular phonic difficulties or to explore particular aspects of phonic knowledge. This technique generally requires the teacher to make a competent phonetic recording of errors and reflects the role of context in word recognition. As already noted, many teachers use simple oral reading attainment tests in just such a way.

An alternative technique suitable for group testing, employed by Carver's *Word Recognition Test* and the *Swansea Test of Phonic Skills*, is to have pupils identify a word dictated by the teacher from a set presented on the test page. The distractors — or 'wrong' alternatives — are so chosen that particular phonic weaknesses will be revealed by wrong choices. Both testing situations are remote from everyday reading tasks, and it must be borne in mind that for some readers the nature and degree of phonic weakness exhibited in such situations may differ from those occurring in his everyday or oral reading. In effect a pupil may successfully read words in context that he cannot read in isolation.

These reservations apart it can be claimed that the testing of phonics has been the area of diagnosis most successfully tackled by test-builders. Published phonic tests can thus be used with greater confidence than other forms of diagnostic tests, provided of course the learner's problems *are* of a phonic kind. One must remember though, that, as with other aspects of reading difficulty, phonic weakness may be an effect of more wide-ranging problems rather than a cause in itself.

Comprehension problems

Some problem readers will have mastered the phonic aspects of reading, but still make little sense of what they read.

This is perhaps one of the most intractable areas of reading difficulty. Fundamental research on the nature of reading comprehension has tended to show that in testing, the greatest part of comprehension ability is accounted for by tests of vocabulary. Poor comprehension would then be associated with a meagre knowledge of word meanings. Further distinctions — of lesser importance — between literal and explicit comprehension and global and inferential understanding have also been made, but in statistical terms they account for very much less.

These elements of comprehension are all dealt with by group tests however. There are no published tests for diagnosis of individual comprehension difficulty. Such diagnosis as can be carried out would

involve use of sub-test scores on group standardized attainment tests —
as described in the sections on the use of profiles. However two
informal techniques must be mentioned:

1. Teacher-made tests: Just because test-based research fails to
uphold the various theoretical descriptions levels and factors in reading
comprehension it does not follow that such distinctions are of no use to
the teacher. Of the schemes that have been developed to describe
comprehension one of the most currently popular is Barrett's Taxonomy (Clymer, 1972) which describes the following categories of
reading comprehension:

- Literal comprehension
- Reorganization
- Inferential comprehension
- Evaluation
- Appreciation

Such a scheme could usefully form the basis for diagnostic testing if
it were to be also the basis for teaching methods and materials. The use
of some form of descriptive scheme, hierarchy or taxonomy can be a
most useful framework or 'working fiction' for diagnosis and teaching.
It will probably meet the needs of the immediate situation much more
effectively than the research evidence might suggest. Although we
might expect tests of various aspects of such a taxonomy or rationale to
be correlated, it does not follow that they are not distinct for teaching
purposes and we cannot assume that, having taught skills in one area or
level, learning will have taken place in all the others with which the
teacher is concerned.

It should be added that whatever the difficulties which have arisen in
testing comprehension skills, they are slight compared to those of
teaching it. Here there has been even less research carried out. Here lies
the difficulty; effective means of measurement are unlikely to
materialize until we have more effective teaching methods. At present
we still do not know enough about the nature of comprehension to
provide effective teaching methods — let alone effective testing
techniques.

2. Cloze tests: The role of the cloze test in assessment of reading
attainment was described in Chapter Four. It also has promise as a
means of individual diagnosis and remedial teaching which has yet to be
fully explored by teachers and researchers.

The idea of cloze procedure is a flexible one, and by the absence of
very much conclusive research evidence the teacher would be free to
construct his test along any lines which suited his own purpose. The

author's own suggestions are as follows:

a) Choose passages of approximately 100 words.
b) Delete roughly every tenth word — but ignore this rule where necessary for commonsense reasons.
c) Delete two or three simple structural words (words necessary for the structure of the sentence, not its meaning, such as 'the', 'for', 'of', 'an' etc.)
d) Delete seven or eight content words (words which convey the meaning and context of sentence — nouns, most verbs etc.)
e) Ensure that all the content words could be discovered by use of context — either because they are used elsewhere in the passage, or because they could be inferred.

Further refinements could include the use of passages at varying levels of readability, the deletion of words from *Keywords to Literacy* as well as less common work, or to classify words in terms of the apparent strength of their contextual cues.

The tests can be administered by having the reader say which word should go in each cloze blank. These are written-in for him by the teacher, but can be crossed out and replaced if the pupil wishes to change his answer.

The reader should be encouraged to think aloud while performing the test. This, together with the kind of errors made will provide much raw material upon which the teacher can base a diagnosis of comprehension difficulty. The following points would merit particular attention:

1. Use of grammatical structure
2. Willingness to scan forward and backwards
3. Capacity to get 'obvious' words
4. Capacity to get less 'obvious' words
5. Ability to reason about guesses
6. Use of author's style (if any) to make guesses
7. Willingness to modify previous answers
8. Ability to use existing knowledge/information outside text to guess words
9. Tendency to get better at test task with practice
10. Ability to retain in memory early parts of passage while attempting later parts

It is possible that research findings will eventually provide the teacher with much clearer and fuller guidelines for the use of cloze procedures. In the meantime the classroom user is free to experiment.

This chapter has discussed the possibilities for diagnosis of the weaknesses or difficulties of backward readers in general. It must be repeated however that where a test reveals areas of weakness of specific difficulty it does not necessarily point to a cause or total explanation of reading failure. In the majority of cases indeed these will be effects, perhaps among many, of more general or intractable problems. An emotionally maladjusted pupil with diagnosed phonic weaknesses, for example, may completely defeat efforts to remedy his phonic weaknesses — the test is not to blame for this!

A diagnostic programme?

The need for a systematic diagnostic programme increases with the severity and variety of reading difficulty being dealt with. A.E. Tansley in *Reading and Remedial Reading* (1967) describes a most thorough and detailed scheme which would be admirable in the special school context, but too unwieldly for use in a junior school or secondary remedial department. It is notable that this scheme makes much more use of specially-devised tests than published ones. While an organized approach to diagnosis is desirable for the class teacher it need not be very elaborate or make extensive use of published materials. It would in any case include considerations of the child's social and cultural background, his temperament and personality and his attitudes and interests in reading. Getting to know the child, and to know about him is itself a most powerful diagnostic process as well as essential for successful teaching.

Devising a diagnostic scheme

There is no one ideal scheme or programme that can be recommended for assessment and diagnosis of reading difficulty. The kinds of problems and the resources available vary considerably from situation to situation and in practice the techniques used for diagnosis vary even in similar situations. A remedial specialist in one school may rely entirely upon his own informal and intuitive judgements, while his counterpart in a similar neighbouring school may make use of a wide variety of materials both published and of his own devising. Yet another teacher may find a simple all-purpose test such as the *Standard Reading Test* appropriate for most of the pupils he has to deal with. There is no evidence to show that one style of diagnosis is ultimately more effective than another. Before embarking on a particular method, however, a teacher could usefully consider the following:

1. *Has the pupil already been tested?* Any policy of assessment to be

carried out in school should take account of existing provision. Precautions should be taken to see that a pupil has not already undergone any formal diagnosis — either by previous teachers or specialist agencies such as Reading Centres or the School Psychological Service. In effect, a *case history* ought to be obtained. If such information is unavailable the teacher should be that much more cautious in putting a child through any 'diagnostic hoops'.

2. *Is there a reading problem?* Diagnostic work should only commence when it is clear the child does have a reading problem. This is most conveniently done by attainment testing. The test selected should reflect the type of reading skill the pupil would be otherwise expected to have. It is pointless, for example, to give a word-recognition test if the schoolwork to follow requires reading for meaning in a more advanced form. The test should also have a sufficient range of difficulty to discriminate between different degrees of reading weakness. Further, the teacher should make sure that a poor readir$_{\circ}$ performance is not, nevertheless the 'best' a child can put up, given any known limitations or ability. The use of an intelligence test is one way of tackling this problem.

3. *What kind of basic diagnosis should follow?* The degree of backwardness in attainment should give some idea of the kind of diagnosis appropriate. Usually the additional information available, such as knowledge of the child's educational history and chronological age will further clarify this.

4. *Is there a perceptual or motor problem?* The younger the child, or the more severe the difficulty the greater the probability that this kind of testing would be appropriate. Whether the teacher uses published materials, devises his own informal tests, or borrows ideas for specialist texts on reading difficulty the following should be considered:

a) Visual perception   (discrimination tasks)

b) Auditory perception   (discrimination tasks)

c) Lateral dominance   (tests of handedness etc.)

d) Eye-hand coordination   (tests of copying)

e) Ocularmotor control   (tests of eye movement)

5. *Is there a problem of memory or sequencing?* These are also considerations which are relevant with younger or more severely retarded readers. In terms of pure memory the teacher should consider the pupil's long-term memory — ability to remember, say, a simple

story — and short-term memory — ability to recall very short strings of letters or numbers and repeat them forwards and backwards. At the same time the accuracy with which the sequence of events, letters or numbers is recalled, should be considered. Tasks based on this principle of sequencing and memory are typical in most pre-reading work, although published tests, such as the Wepman's *Tests of Auditory and Visual Sequential Memory* provide a convenient published instrument. The user of these particular tests should perhaps note that the author does not claim any dramatic relationship between poor performance on these tests and reading difficulty.

6. *Is the problem conceptual?* A comprehensive review of research into reading difficulty by M.D. Vernon (1957) suggested that underlying many studies was the implication that the pupils were basically confused about the purpose and nature of reading — yet this is not an area of difficulty which has been catered for very fully by tests. To some extent reading readiness tests which emphasize word-picture matching would seem to reflect this problem — general tests of mental development may also be pertinent. Marie Clay's *Concepts About Print Test (Sand)* (1972) also tests the child's understanding of the conventions of the printed word and covers both understanding of the function of print in conveying meaning and the conventions governing the way words are printed, such as left-to-right direction and punctuation. It is perhaps one of the most promising methods for assessing a child's conceptual grasp of the purpose and nature of the written word.

7. *Is the problem one of word attack or phonics?* The pupil's age, educational history and attainment test performance may suggest he needs systematic training in decoding skills. Alternatively he may have successfully performed the perceptual and motor tasks, but still not show very much headway in decoding ability. In this case a survey of his existing phonic knowledge should be made. It should be noted however that where difficulty is encountered in the early stages of testing — letter recognition, blending of sounds in simple three-letter words — testing should be discontinued and teaching should commence. There is no point in going on with the test. If thought desirable the pupil can be tested on the more difficult parts at a later stage. Tests such as the *Domain Test of Phonic Skills* should most definitely be handled in this way.

Because such thorough means of phonic testing — and teaching — are available it is easy to assume this approach is suitable for all reading problems in the junior and middle years of schooling. The teacher should strive to establish that it really is the case that the reader just cannot 'break the code', and needs training in this, rather than in using all the other kinds of cues available to the reader.

8. *Is the problem one of comprehension?* The problem of the child who can decode but cannot make much sense of what he reads has already been mentioned. In spite of the interest of research workers relatively little is known about the diagnosis and remediation of comprehension difficulty. There seem to be fewer practical texts published on the subject. As a result the individual teacher is very much obliged to use his own judgement in drawing on theories of comprehension, and testing and teaching materials to produce his own scheme of assessment.

9. *Is the problem associated with untestable factors?* It has been stressed throughout this chapter that tests have only a partial role in diagnostic teaching and that even in situations where they are appropriate their use is not mandatory. The example of many skilled teachers of reading shows as much. Further, it would be impossible to pretend that the causes and antecedents of many reading problems are of a simple testable variety. This is certainly the most important question to have in mind in attempting to appraise a pupil's reading problems.

The Aston Index (M. Newton and M. Thomson)

For some years research has been going on at the Department of Applied Psychology of the University of Aston, Birmingham into specific reading difficulty. Part of this work has been the development of a series of tests designed to identify young children likely to have fundamental difficulty in learning to read (Form I) and to cast light on puzzling cases of reading failure in older children (Form II). A further more probing set of tests to be used by specialists for children who are referred with severe disability (Form III) is also under development. Forms I and II of these tests — *The Aston Index* are being developed for use by teachers. The experimental forms are of interest in that they bring together in one package many of the test-techniques mentioned in this and previous chapters. Form I for example contains four main sections:

1. General Underlying Ability: (Picture recognition; Vocabulary; Draw-a-man test, copying designs).
2. General Background factors with emphasis upon lateral dominance.
3. Tests of child's laterality.
4. Performance Tests: (Writing and Copying, Visual and Auditory Sequential memory; sound blending, sound discrimination).

Form II contains these tests but includes Schonell's graded spelling and word-recognition tests, samples of the child's free writing and a graphomotor test for assessing general motor control and dominant handedness.

The tests are noteworthy, not only because they bring together many techniques which have customarily been used more by psychologists than teachers, but for their emphasis on neurological factors in reading difficulty, particularly laterality which is investigated in some depth.

The Index is still in the process of validation and although the body of research which has already been carried out is promising the authors are careful not to make any categorical claims for the validity of the Index or about the nature of specific reading difficulty.

The tests themselves certainly illustrate the point that has already been made about the need to base all testing on a full knowledge and understanding of the theoretical and research background. Without this, the Index is unlikely to be very much use to a teacher.

Chapter Nine

Criterion-referenced testing and item banking

The kinds of tests discussed in this book so far have been either diagnostic, as discussed in the previous chapter, or norm-referenced in that they are used to compare a child with some kind of standard or norm.

For some time however test theorists — particularly in the United States — have been interested in the concept of criterion-referenced testing. Different interpretations of this term have been made, but in general it applies to kinds of tests which measure how much or what a child has learned in a particular school subject or skill area. Thus while norm-referenced tests take an average standard as their point of reference, criterion-referenced tests take the mastery of a particular piece of learning as their point of reference. In theory a criterion-referenced test constructor is concerned with building a test which closely reflects the content of what is to be learned and not with measuring how much worse or better one pupil is than another. The test is not designed to produce a 'normal' distribution of test scores, but rather to divide pupils into two groups — those who have reached a minimal level of competence, and those that have not.

This reflects differences in the way in which criterion-referenced tests are used. A norm-referenced test is essentially a measure of how much a pupil has learned, relative to others, after a period of teaching and learning. Such a period is usually a long one, perhaps a term, a year or even a school career. The evaluation which takes place here is *summative*, it sums up as it were the effectiveness of all the teaching that has gone before. A pupil's score tells us little directly about what he *can or cannot do*, only that whatever he can do, he does it better or worse than a known proportion of other children. In fact we will know generally the area of reading to which his score refers, say word-recognition or comprehension, but little beyond this.

By contrast, a criterion-referenced test score might consist of a whole detailed inventory of skills which a pupil has or has not mastered. These inventories are made during the process of teaching and on their basis the decisions are made about giving more instruction and practice in a particular skill, or moving the child on to more advanced work. As the testing takes place during the course of teaching it is sometimes called *formative* evaluation. The principle is simply the one of teaching, testing and providing further teaching or re-teaching as necessary. Much informal day to day classroom testing is in this formative spirit rather than in a summative one — like an end-of-term examination.

Much of the published criterion-referenced test material has been produced as part of a highly structured package or kit of programmed teaching materials of a kind not widely used in British schools. SRA and similar reading laboratories are perhaps the closest examples of this approach available in Britain.

In principle the idea of criterion-referenced testing is an attractive one: it is in line with the way teachers have always carried out testing in their classrooms and it has a strongly diagnostic leaning — phonic tests such as the *Standard Reading Test* or *Get Reading Right* are clearly criterion-referenced even though they do not say so. However in practice it has been little less than disastrous! The essence of a criterion-referenced test is a rationale or mapping-out of the reading skills to be learned so that criterial test items can be produced. The result has been the production of long and spurious lists of skills to be mastered — which implies that they should each be specifically taught — in a way which has little to do with what we know about the way the reading process operates or reading skill is acquired. In effect, the test constructors have tended to make a great number of wholly unjustified assumptions about the way children can be taught to read.

For example, the tests of Reading Comprehension Skills (K-6) produced by the Instructional Objectives Exchange (1973) in Los Angeles cover all the following skills:

Main idea
Finding common attributes
Identifying main ideas of pictures
Identifying the most general
    statement
Finding the moral
Finding the factual generalization

Conclusions
Identifying the probable outcome of
    a pictured situation
Simple logical reasoning
Identifying the cause of a simple
    event

Conclusions (Cont.)
Identifying the cause of a detailed
    event
Identifying situations from
    information
Identifying causal relationships based
    on agreement and difference
Identifying possible outcomes
Drawing conclusions about
    occupation, character, and
    locality
Making deductions from factual
    information
Identifying the writer's point of view

Sequence
Determining first and last in temporal
    sequence
Ordering events and instructions
Determining sequence on the basis of
    logical dependency
Determining sequence from tense and
    words that signal order
Arranging sentences in narrative
    order
Rearranging sentences from
    flash-back or flash-ahead sequence
    to chronological sequence
Identifying the dramatic functions of
    paragraphs

Context clues
Subject pronoun referents —
    matching pictures to pronouns
Subject pronoun referents —
    matching nouns to pronouns
Subject and object pronoun referents
Subject, object and demonstrative
    pronoun referents
Indefinite, demonstrative and
    possessive pronoun referents
Selecting examples and synonyms to
    match contextual definitions
Deriving meaning of unfamiliar letter
    combinations
Deriving the meaning of an
    unfamiliar word
Deriving meaning of an unfamiliar
    word given more than one
    possible definition

Punctuation
Matching punctuation with
    intonation
Identifying sentences with ellipse,
    titles, restrictive and
    non-restrictive clauses, and
    emphasis
Determining sentence meaning from
    comma, italics, quotation and
    other marks

Syntactical structures
Understanding explicitly-stated
    content
Selecting opposites of negative
    statements
Interpreting passive and active voice
Interpreting complex sentences

Affixes
Prefixes
Suffixes

What is involved in each skill and the methods for assessing it are described very fully. However while there is some virtue in being so explicit about what is actually being taught and tested many of the divisions are arbitrary and are really only manifestations of other underlying skills.

The dubiousness of all this would become painfully apparent to the test constructors if they made efforts to find out what relation performance on their tests have to mastery of the supposed sub-skills in real life. For the most part however they prefer to set on arbitrary score as the criterion score to indicate mastery of a skill. Customarily this has been chosen as 80 per cent, and it must be taken on trust that child who scores 80 per cent or more can actually *do* whatever it is that is being tested.

The moral is that criterion-referenced testing will only be usefully applied to areas where there is a good understanding of the way things should be taught and where it makes sense to carry out a schematic analysis of the content of teaching.

Phonic tests are thus a good example of criterion-referenced testing. For example, a child who fails to read a word (or set of words) involving vowel-blends can be said to have 'failed to master' this aspect of phonics. Accordingly quite specific exercises and practices can be given. Some doubts must remain however. Is it fair to diagnose a specific phonic difficulty on the basis of one or two words containing vowel-blends? Statistically such a test will be unreliable. Further we must take it on trust — though not unreasonably — that a child who fails vowel-blend test items will probably have wide ranging vowel-blending difficulties in daily reading.

At present few of the American criterion-referenced tests based upon doubtful conceptions of reading are being marketed in Britain. The danger they represent is thus a remote one, and hopefully British teachers will be able to make use of the extremely valuable principle of testing what a child *knows*, rather than just his relative superiority or inferiority, in ways which are not so widely at odds with what we know about the way reading can be taught. One way this could happen would be by teachers themselves experimenting with the utility and validity of criterion tests of their own devising as part of their day to day teaching.

Item banking

Recently there has been considerable interest in the notion of item or question banking. Test construction agencies often assemble such banks as a matter of course, and select from them to produce 'set-piece' tests. Item banking in the form of books of examples has been with us for many years, though not primarily for assessment purposes. The distinction between these examples and the modern use of item banks is mainly one of sophistication of techniques of both test construction and item analysis.

It is often felt that the sort of tests which are widely available in which every pupil must attempt every question are unduly restrictive. Although this point can be overstated, it is undoubtedly the case that constructors must play safe when assembling a new test. Tests which are intended for general usage over a wide range of ability and perhaps age (as well as a variety of teaching approaches) must be limited to a closely defined core of material since otherwise pupils could be confronted with questions for which they were completely unprepared. The corollary of this is that such tests cannot possibly reflect every nuance of local interest and individual teaching method. Another problem which arises with straightforward standardized tests is that of age. Not only can the standardization data become out-of-date, so that they no longer reflect national or local standards, but the *content* of the test can also suffer in this way. The techniques of item banking provide at least partial solutions to these problems.

It might seem from the foregoing that the construction of an item bank is a simple task. All that appears necessary is for a few hundred items to be written, tried out and published! This is, of course, very far from the truth. In many ways an item bank requires a more considered approach than a traditional test. In the case of ordinary tests, a test constructor is often concerned with an explicitly stated, but limited, sub-skill or a larger field of knowledge or behaviour. There are rare occasions when an item bank might be limited in a similar way, but usually it will range further afield than a single test. It is therefore important for the item bank writer to have a clear overview of the attainment with which he is concerned.

A curriculum or content analysis is a prerequisite for any serious work on the construction of an item bank. Once this analysis is complete, a blueprint can be drawn for the bank. A purely theoretical scheme or taxonomy of reading skills could be used, alternatively the blueprint could be made to reflect either the stages through which reading ability develops or the dimensions of a skill, such as comprehension, which have been identified in research work.

It is not necessary for every category in such a blueprint to be filled, but the blueprint approach ensures that even the most idiosyncratic item bank user is unlikely to be disappointed. When the items have been written to fit the blueprint they are analysed (at least in the initial stages) in the way outlined in Chapter Two.

Item banks, then, are constructed after extensive curriculum and item analysis and are considerably more flexible than traditional tests. The principal advantage of this flexibility is the freedom which it allows the user to match the test to the pupils. Each item in a bank carries with it not only statistical information but also details of the cell in the blueprint which it occupies, and item banks are often considered criterion (or content) referenced for this reason. Local factors and individual emphases of teaching can thus be taken into account, and the bank can be kept up-to-date by discarding old items and replacing them with modified or even completely new ones.

Why then have item banks not replaced the more traditional set-piece test? The answer is three-fold: firstly, item banking *as such* is still a relatively new idea; secondly, item banks can be inconvenient. Hand in hand with the increased flexibility of the item bank approach comes the requirement for users to select the items. This can be tedious, and it may be necessary for the user to arrange for compilation and duplication of the test. Computerization can help to overcome these problems but according to a recent report *Computerised Question Banking Systems* by C.J. Byrne (1975) there are still only about 100 computerized item bank systems in use in the world; only one is in England.

Finally there is the problem of test reliability and comparability. No matter how meticulously an item bank is constructed, the lack of control over the final test (which is inevitable if the advantages of item banking are to be fully exploited) makes it more difficult to achieve high reliability values. In addition it is clear that some allowance must be made for the fact that the items in the bank will not be of equal difficulty. A score on a test made up of the 20 easiest items cannot be directly compared with a score gained on the 20 most difficult ones. There are a number of ways of determining weights for the items, but most of them are beyond the scope of this book. Perhaps the most obvious and for many purposes the most satisfactory method is to weight the items according to the proportion of candidates in a representative sample who answer them correctly. A score on any set of items from the bank can then be related to the score which the representative sample would have achieved, and a means of standardizing the bank is available.

The advantages of item banking for the individual teacher are clear. Rather than accepting a ready made test, he can construct his own to meet his own requirements, yet still obtain a nationally meaningful score. Item banking is also a useful tool for larger scale surveys, such as those sometimes undertaken by local education authorities. For example, schools involved in the survey can choose tests from the bank which suit their own approach to reading more closely than is possible with externally constructed tests. The data from these tests can still be pooled to provide meaningful authority-wide statistics, but with greater certainty that the tests are valid for the pupils assessed.

As has already been said, item banking is a relatively new idea. For the reasons outlined in this chapter it is likely to be of increasing importance in the future; however, it is doubtful whether item banks will replace traditional standardized tests. A set-piece test is adequate for many purposes and is more convenient than even a computerized item bank. In addition it will be some years yet before the high reliabilities which are routinely obtained for standardized tests are so easily achieved with item banks.

Chapter Ten

Informal test procedures

Most of the tests which were described in the preceding chapters have been of the objective variety — after they have been standardized nearly all are published *as* tests, rather than as part of a book or scheme. Many books on the teaching of reading include the writer's own suggestions on how reading progress and abilities or difficulties can be assessed. While such methods lie outside the main interests of this book their usefulness to the teacher should not be underestimated.

We have already mentioned two techniques, cloze procedure and the Informal Reading Inventory which come into this category. Mention has also been made of A.E. Tansley's suggestions in *Reading and Remedial Reading* (1958) for a very full scheme of diagnosis of fundamental reading difficulties.

There are some more recent writers who have made interesting suggestions for testing methods. John M. Hughes, for example, in *Reading and Reading Failures* (1975) makes a number of practical suggestions about the way listening and auditory and visual functioning can be examined. This writer favours a systematic phonic approach and provides a thorough guide to the testing of phonic skills. In addition to remarks on how to assess word-attack skills he presents a more formal phonic test in seven sections, ranging from initial vowel and consonants to digraphs and dipthongs. The test is similar in principle to the Carver and Swansea tests in that the pupil has to identify the correct graphemic — reprinted — representation of a phoneme — i.e. a 'spoken' sound.

The test consists of 90 items, all in the form of five printed nonsense words, one of which will correspond to that spoken out by the tester. The test is designed to be used in conjunction with other books by the author on phonic teaching. As a simple guide to be used informally within the classroom Hughes' approach, and others like it, have much to recommend them. A teacher who just occasionally has to assess a particular child in a slightly more systematic form than can be done on

an *ad hoc* basis need rarely look further than procedures of this type. A very much fuller development of the informal approach is suggested by Dan and Nichols in *Framework for Reading* (1974) in which a series of checklists and test tasks are provided to chart progress throughout the pre-reading and early reading stages. A second set of tests is included for the assessment of pupils in making satisfactory progress.

The first checklist guides the teacher's observation of the child through two levels of development:

Level 1. Understanding the language of instruction
          Word recognition
          Handwriting skills
          Analysis of word patterns
          Early phonic knowledge
Level 2. Development of reading skills (word attack and observation)
          More advanced phonic knowledge
          Emergence of difficulties

Each test or series of points to be checked is backed-up by guidance on materials and techniques which would be appropriate to develop the skills under consideration.

The second list guides the teacher to observe and test the child's motivations, language skills and auditory, visual and motor development. Again, advice is given on the appropriate remedial teaching to be given in each area.

This particular scheme could be used as the basis of a systematic record keeping scheme as an alternative to traditional test-based methods of recording progress in school. It has the virtues of being comprehensive and closely relates teaching and testing. To use it in full might prove cumbersome, particularly with large groups of children, and some of the points to be checked off perhaps rely heavily upon the subjective judgement of the teachers.

Schemes of this sort have the makings of a viable alternative to standardized testing as an assessment policy within the classroom, or perhaps within the whole school. Further even when there is a definite need for normative assessment of reading there is every advantage in supplementing it with data from systematically kept recordings of observations made within a framework of this kind.

A very different application of informal methods is provided by Marie M. Clay in her *Diagnostic Survey* for the early detection of reading difficulty. The survey is intended for the diagnosis of reading difficulty at the age of six years. In addition to the informal methods of diagnosis the survey includes some specially prepared test materials for which some limited normative data are presented. The approach has characteristics of both the Informal Reading Inventory and standardized testing.

In all, five areas of testing are covered:

1. *A running record*: A technique is described in which a record is made of the accuracy with which the child reads a sample of 100 to 200 words from his current reader. This is assessed for accuracy (one error in any three running words of text is described as poor) and for self-correction (a self-correction rate of one in three or one in five errors is good). Further, advice is given on the observations and analysis of the pupil's sense of directionality — i.e. ability to deal with the 'left to right' running of words and sentences.

2. *Letter identification*: This is a printed test containing all the letters of the alphabet in upper and lower case. The child is asked to name each letter. Particular attention is to be paid to the child's style of responding, for example, providing the name of the letter or an acceptable corresponding sound.

3. *Concepts about print ('SAND')*: This test comes in the form of a printed booklet which looks very like an ordinary reader. However, it is the basis of some 24 test items, ranging from the child's ability to identify the cover of a book and correctly orientate it, to concepts about letter order and punctuation. The key items are those which deal with the child's understanding that print is used to convey meaning and that it is governed by rules of order and sequence. The test tasks do not require the child to do any reading himself, although interestingly some of the questions are not correctly answered by more than 50 per cent of 'average' seven-year-olds.

4. *'Ready to read' word test*: This is a test of reading vocabulary accumulated in the first year of reading instruction. As it is of necessity based on a particular reading scheme its general use will be limited, although it may serve as an example for teachers who wish to make their own word recognition tests.

Reliability values for most of the assessment techniques are provided, together with norms based on relatively small samples of children tested in 1968. Only the reliability for recording self-correction appears to be suspect, and high correlations of the tests with a word reading test are quoted. Advice on the use of other reading tests and the assessment of the child's written language is included in the test, together with examples of how some of the techniques of analysis can be applied to the *Neale Analysis of Reading Ability*.

The *Diagnostic Survey* is too new for there to be much information about how useful teachers find it in practice. However it is a promising example of the way future reading tests could develop. New and potentially illuminating techniques for diagnosis are emphasized rather than the statistical background to the tests. The methods recommended by Marie Clay are part of a larger body of research by this author into the development of reading strategies and some familiarity with this work, particularly *Reading: The Patterning of Complex Behaviour* (1972) would be helpful. Clay's work is similar to that of Kenneth and Yetta Goodman in that it is concerned with the cues children use when reading. Indeed a *Reading Miscues Inventory* (Goodman and Burke, 1970) has been produced which provides a rationale for the analysis and interpretation of children's reading errors. This too has the makings of an informal test, although it is difficult to obtain in Britain.

Finally, in this discussion of informal approaches to reading assessment the radically different approach discussed by Herbert Kohl in *Reading, How To* (1974) should be mentioned. Kohl is opposed to standardized objective testing of the kind described in this book, although it must be realized he is reacting against wholesale and rigid testing practices in American schools and the overspecific and literal use of reading tests. Kohl describes four levels of reading development which he calls 'Beginning', 'Not bad', 'With ease' and 'Complex'. At each level there are a number of skills and levels of understanding and performance that the teacher should be sensitive to (Figure 10A). These are based on Kohl's own experiences and beliefs about the teaching of reading. The rating of a pupil's standing on any of the points in the chart is a subjective matter and Kohl is at pains to stress that his chart is not a system for teaching reading which embodies absolute truths about learning to read. He grudgingly admits however that it could be used as a means of recording group and individual progress over some time, and indeed for some of the evaluative purposes normally served by standardized tests. Like *Framework for Reading* it has potential as an alternative to testing and it would lend itself easily to personal modification or to more detailed development, although Kohl himself firmly warns against the latter. The chart is sufficiently useful and informative to justify its use on a slightly more official basis than Kohl would perhaps recommend, either as a supplement to standardized testing or, for those who wish it, a complete alternative.

The methods of assessment described in this chapter are not as statistically 'respectable' as the kinds of tests we have been primarily concerned with throughout this book. Yet it is clear that informal techniques often contain some of the best material from the reading teacher's point of view. Further, they do have the potential for fuller statistical development. If they had attracted the energy and resources which have been expended on conventional reading tests in the past they might by now be in a much more advanced form. Hopefully the test constructors of the future will have sufficient imagination to

Figure 10A: A Chart of Reading Progress

		Understanding			Physical Conditioning		
	Skills	Confidence	Strategy	Street understanding	Book understanding	Speed	Stamina
Beginning	1. Knowing print 2. Known words 3. Words that connect and words 4. Alphabet 5. Sounds and combinations of sounds 6. Simple sentences	None Not much Enough	Panics Evades Copes Deals	Not at all With problems OK	Not at all With problems OK	Very slow Slow OK Speed freak	No stamina Problems with stamina OK Stamina freak
Not bad	1. Combinations of sounds 2. Complicated words 3. Complex sentences 4. Everyday reading 5. Paragraphs and stories	None Not much Enough	Panics Evades Copes Deals	Not at all With problems OK	Not at all With problems OK	Very slow Slow OK Speed freak	No stamina Problems with stamina OK Stamina freak
With ease	1. Unfamiliar words 2. Different forms of writing 3. Voice 4. Test taking	None Not much Enough	Panics Evades Copes Deals	Not at all With problems OK	Not at all With problems OK	Very slow Slow OK Speed freak	No stamina Problems with stamina OK Stamina freak
Complex	1. Knowing about language 2. Special uses of words 3. Special languages 4. Critical analysis	None Not much Enough	Panics Evades Copes Deals	Not at all With problems OK	Not at all With problems OK	Very slow Slow OK Speed freak	No stamina Problems with stamina OK Stamina freak

From *Reading How To*, Kohl, (1974), pp. 126–127. Harmondsworth: Penguin. Reprinted by permission of Penguin Books Ltd.

appreciate this. In the meantime, the teacher of reading should always be on the lookout for useful innovations in the field of informal assessment and should not assume that they will be less suited to his testing purposes than other forms of test.

Chapter Eleven

Practical problems

This chapter deals with some of the common practical problems which arise in the use of reading tests. The suggestions we make are not sacred. In particular circumstances the professional judgement of the teacher on the spot might overrule some of them, or the demands of the situation might sometimes justify a different approach. For the most part though, they are guides which should not be ignored without careful thought beforehand.

Should extra time be permitted for completion of a test?

Some test manuals specify a strict time limit, others are a little more vague or less adamant about this. Technically, tests can be divided into speed tests and power tests. A speed test involves doing as many questions as possible against the clock. The test is designed to see how far a task can be performed and how many tasks can be completed in the same time by readers of different abilities. NFER Reading Test EH-3 is a typical speed test. The individual test tasks are not very hard but it would, on the other hand, be very difficult for the average 12-year-old to complete them all in the short time allowed. Similarly, a very early test of reading, the *Ballard One Minute Reading Test* (Ballard, 1960) just required the pupil to read as many unrelated words as he could from a list in one minute. In speed tests the time limit is of extreme importance if the norms are to apply — the whole point of the test rests on the time factor. By the criterion of such tests the 'slower' and 'less able' readers are synonymous. Speed is what differentiates between testees and creates a spread or distribution of ability. Where the test is clearly a speeded one the time limit must therefore be observed literally and strictly.

Most tests of reading are however power tests. These tests aim to distribute the pupils in terms of the intrinsic difficulty of individual questions. A time limit is however often set for such tests and the assumption is made that anyone who had not finished within that time would have in fact got no further questions correct anyway. The statistics behind power tests usually presuppose that all testees have had the opportunity to attempt all the questions. The time limit is added on afterwards as a guide to teachers who wish to use the test within the practical limits upon time encountered in schools. Such a time limit will probably have been used in standardization work, and the norms may thus contain an element of speed in them. Observation of the time limit is probably not so crucial as in speed tests, but it is desirable that it is observed as far as possible. Where it is clear that a child or group has been penalized by time limits another test — more generous in its time allowance — could be given. Alternatively, test papers can be marked with an identifier at the question reached at the time limit and the test can then be continued — *without amendment to prior answers* until pupils have done as much as they can. Two marks can then be recorded for each child, so that the effect of the time limit, if any, can be observed.

Classroom organization

Test manuals invariably prescribe examination conditions of testing which usually require pupils to be seated at separate desks and may even require two teachers to be present in the classroom to invigilate the test. Yet many schools, particularly primary schools, cannot meet these requirements because of the architecture of the school or because extra staff are just not available. Doing the 'best one can' does not invalidate testing however, provided that a *minimum* level of conditions can be met. The most important condition — and the most difficult to meet*— is avoidance of cooperative working and copying of answers. Other physical conditions are not so crucial providing they at least allow the children working conditions to which they are used and which avoid any gross disturbances or distractions.

Guessing

A problem associated with multiple-choice testing is that of the 'test sophisticated' pupil who answers questions which are really too hard for him in the hope of picking up a few more marks through sheer luck. Some tests allow for this by instructing that marking should cease after a given number of consecutive wrong answers. Where this adjustment is not permitted and extreme cases of guessing are suspected there is a simple commonsense approach which can be applied: where the pupil's score is less than he would get by guessing (usually about one in five as tests usually use this number of alternative answers) and he picks up as many marks in harder parts of the test as in the easier part his score should be discounted. Even though he may have earned some marks through genuine reading the test will have been generally too hard to permit useful interpretation of his result.

It is less easy to advise in the case of a pupil who has appeared to boost his score by randomly completing just the harder items, having already earned a mark above the chance level. Even if it seems possible to detect this phenomenon it is not a good idea to alter the child's score as this would violate the objectivity of the test. It would be better to employ a second test, less prone to random guessing, to confirm that the first score is really open to serious question.

Practice and revision of test papers

In theory, every reading lesson is 'practice' for a test, but teachers may be anxious because a particular format of questioning found in a test is sufficiently unfamiliar to spuriously confuse pupils. There is accordingly, a temptation to do a few dummy runs sometime before the test proper. Unless the teaching which is involved here is indisputably worthwhile in its own right, such preparation is unjustified and tends to invalidate the test results. Nearly all tests include practice examples intended to familiarize pupils adequately with the particular style of questioning adopted and to eliminate bias in results from this source.

While one must be honest and admit that differences in test performances are partly influenced by sheer test-taking ability, as well as reading ability, there is no evidence to show that coaching eliminates this or leads to a somehow 'truer' set of results. At the same time, it must be realized that reading tests are used on a regular basis in many schools, and norms for most tests will be based largely on children who have had some experience of the test situation. Pupils who happen to be totally unfamiliar with the experience of being tested can thus be expected to be at least at a slight disadvantage when doing their first reading test. A difference of this kind can certainly be taken into account when interpreting the results. Rarely however, will a practice or 'mock' testing session be justified.

The benefits of 'going through' a reading test after it has been done have not been researched, although a few tests indeed do recommend such a procedure. This practice would seem to be inadvisable if any further testing is planned in the near future and should certainly not be carried out with a version of a test which is to be re-used. If the test has merit as a teaching material in its own right — for example a cloze test — then by all means let it be used as such provided the exercise does not degenerate to a coaching programme.

Exclusion of particular children from testing

Teachers are sometimes faced with the decision either to inflict a stressful testing session on a non-reader or to single out the child by excluding him from the test. Neither course is really desirable. One may be able to 'slip' an easier test to some less able readers (NFER Tests for example are superficially very similar in appearance, although the practice examples may have to be altered for smooth group testing). One might alternatively test two halves or groups of a class on different days and contrive to have special pupils in the non-tested half on both occasions. There is no reason why some children should not attempt a reading test while the remainder of a class are left to do some quiet work. If at all possible, the necessity to either test *or* exclude very backward children should be avoided.

Marking keys

Occasionally it may appear in a multiple-choice test that an alternative answer to that keyed as correct would be acceptable. In most instances the allowance of the alternative makes no real difference to the results. We strongly advise against relaxation of the marking key. Insistence upon the official answer will in all probability, be a more effective means of discriminating between the more and less able readers.

In oral or more open-ended tests an element of judgement is inevitably involved in marking. Here effective assessment requires some skill on the part of the teachers involved. This can best be assured by arranging for practice testing and discussion of tape recorded test performances before testing proper commences. The users of such tests should in any case appreciate that they are often inclined to be less reliable than more objective forms of testing.

Accuracy of marking

Under ideal circumstances a test paper should be marked twice by independent markers. People vary in the accuracy with which they can mark tests, however hard they may concentrate. When large numbers of scripts are involved it may suffice to re-mark a ten per cent sample, and only re-mark the complete batch if more than one question in 100 is incorrectly scored, unless the error is a consistent one, in which case complete re-marking should still take place. Any individual results should certainly be double-checked before they are interpreted or a crucial diagnosis is attempted. This checking rule applies not only to marking but to any other clerical operation such as calculation of dates of birth or conversion of raw scores to a scale. The practice of having children mark their own scripts is definitely not to be encouraged. Some commercial concerns and test producers offer mechanical or electronic test-marking facilities to their customers. Such services are generally expensive and require very large numbers of test papers (usually specially printed) before they become economically viable, in any case it would be essential to discuss such a possibility with the agency concerned well before testing is to take place.

Some labour may be saved by fabrication of one's own marking guide in the form of a card template or perspex overlay along the lines of those produced commercially. This can be marked out to act as a guide to the marker's eye and thus save some effort. An overhead projector transparency can be used in this way, but one should be absolutely sure that such a device can be used accurately.

Reproduction of Test Materials

Like any other printed matter test materials are copyright and the permission of the authors and publishers must be obtained before any copying — even in part — is carried out. Once this was done, great care would have to be taken to ensure that the copy was visually as close to the original as possible. Publishers themselves sometimes make slight amendments in the printed format of their tests. Such changes are however usually kept at a minimum and great care is taken to avoid making the test either substantially harder or *easier* because this might jeopardize the relevance of the norm. Reading is in important respects a visual perceptual process, and the legibility of the printed media employed is therefore crucial. This is particularly important in respect of tests which make use of the pictorial content, or are intended for younger pupils.

Economies

Test materials are not always produced in the most economical form possible. For example, a test paper may be designed so that it cannot be re-used because the testee has to write on it.

One of the authors carried out a piece of research in 1974 to see if it was practical to modify existing testing materials to make them re-useable. This involved testing all seven-year-olds in a single local authority. The test used was a sentence reading test very similar in difficulty and visual layout to NFER Reading Test A. Ten per cent of the children were asked to record their answers by circling a number on a separate sheet. The rest of the sample circled the word or phrase to complete a sentence on the actual test paper. The results for the 'separate answer sheet' children were almost identical in terms of the mean distribution of scores to those who answered in the normal way. These results suggest that a separate answer sheet system might be adopted for other tests along similar lines, without bringing into question the appropriateness of the existing norms.

These seven-year-olds were in fact better readers for their age than seven-year-olds nationally, and the result in no way can be taken as carte blanche for teachers to produce their own answer sheets for tests

indiscriminately. Great care and thought should go into the design stages of such an enterprise. The layout of the answer sheet is crucial, as it may introduce new perceptual memory and clerical operations for the child. It would also be highly desirable that the modified format should be pre-tried and compared with the official method of answering before any large-scale testing is carried out. This line of work however is one which larger schools with fairly full testing programmes could fruitfully develop.

Communication of results to parents

One important ethical question concerns the way in which results of a reading test are used in discussions with parents. Some teachers do quote actual reading ages or quotients to parents, either to reassure them or to bring their concern and involvement.

Hopefully our previous discussion of what test scores actually mean will have convinced the reader that they need a deal of qualification and placing in context if they are to be truthfully interpreted. It would always be preferable to present parents with the meanings and implications of a test result rather than a 'naked' test score. 'Johnny only has a reading age of eight', can be a dramatic but misleading – and mischievious – piece of news to a parent. It would have been better by far to say that Johnny had failed to reach the normal level for this age (by perhaps quite a long way) or was reading less well than 75 per cent of children of his age, and less well than 85 per cent of his class. It is always more useful to think – and talk – in terms of the information contained in a test result rather than to use the test result as a literal label. We would thus advise the exercise of some professional discretion in quoting a test result to parents.

Chapter Twelve

Published tests

In this chapter a representative selection of reading tests is described. The choice has been limited to tests which are readily available to teachers in Britain. This usually means that the tests have either been standardized for British children, or that they can be used without specialized training. In the selection the emphasis is upon reading tests rather than tests of other language skills. A number of such tests are available, notably the NFER *English Progress Tests* and Nelson's *Bristol Achievement Series: English Language*, but all the tests in each series are very similar in format and in any case the value of their content is rather questionable.

The descriptive reviews of tests are followed by tables which contain supplementary information about the technical characteristics of the tests. The dates of construction given apply to the approximate year of standardization, or to the year in which the test was developed if no norms are available.

The reliability values given have been divided into the 'internal consistency' types and 'test re-test' types. The latter type will of course tend to be a little lower than the former. They include values based on the correlations between equivalent forms of a test. In some cases the standard errors quoted are based on the authors' own estimations and their accuracy cannot be entirely vouched for.

The time limits given are only a rough guide as some tests are really untimed while others consist of a number of separate parts to be administered in different sessions.

The score scales are usually given as either reading ages (RAs), percentiles or standardized scores (SS). Some manuals give scores as quotients or deviation quotients, in fact these are usually standardized scores.

We would not recommend the decision to use any of these tests be made without inspection of the actual test beforehand. It is usually possible to obtain inspection or specimen copies from the publishers for this purpose. In many cases tests cannot be purchased through bookshops and the buyer must apply directly to the publishers.

Attainment tests

Assessment of Reading Ability
D. Labon West Sussex County Council

This booklet was produced by West Sussex School Psychological Service and contains both basic advice about the diagnosis of reading difficulty and a set of five diagnostic tests. The tests to be given are selected on the basis of the child's reading age on the Schonell GWRT (included in the booklet) and advice is provided about the kind of teaching which should follow testing. Basically the tests enable the teacher to decide whether the child would benefit from pre-phonic or phonic teaching. The tests might therefore be described as tests of 'phonic readiness':

1. *Letter Shapes*: This is a very simple test of visual discrimination in which the child has to sort the letters 'a', 'b', 'c', 'd' and 'e' which are written on separate cards. A similar exercise is performed with 'v', 'w', 'x', 'y' and 'z'.
2. *Word Pairs*: This is a simple 12-item version of the Wepman Auditory Discrimination Test.
3. *Letter-Sounds*: This is simply a test of letter-sound knowledge. The instructions point out that even children who have in other respects reached the stage of phonic readiness often fail to know the sounds of all the letters of the alphabet.
4. *Odd-Man Out*: This is a more searching test of auditory discrimination in which the 'odd-man out' of five spoken words has to be identified by the child, for example, 'shout-sharp-shell-gun'.
5. *Word-Building*: This is a test of nonsense-word recognition. The 45 words are chosen — as in tests like the Swansea Test — to represent common phonic elements. This is a more demanding test than the others, and is suitable for children who have mastered the phonic skils covered in the other tests, but are still having particular difficulties.

The tests are intended for use in conjunction with activities described in other booklets produced by the West Sussex Psychological Service, and the test materials are all produced by the teacher himself. Although the tests were particularly intended for use by teachers in West Sussex they evidently have a much wider application and provide a cheap and convenient way of applying techniques which are central to diagnosis.

Burt (Rearranged) Graded Word Reading Test, ULP
C. Burt and P.E. Vernon

This is a conventional GWRT which was originally standardized by Sir Cyril Burt in 1921 but was amended by P.E. Vernon in 1938 using Scottish children. Norms for 6044 Cheshire children tested in 1972 are available from the NFER,[1] although this standardization study revealed that in any case the order of difficulty of items had changed. A similar re-standardization exercise has been carried out by the Scottish Council for Educational Research, which seems a pity in view of the basically archaic conception of reading underlying the tests.

Edinburgh Reading Tests Stage 2, ULP
Godfrey Thompson Unit, University of Edinburgh

The test consists of five sub-tests:

a. *Vocabulary: 1)* Sentence-completion 2) Selection of synonyms for underlined words in sentences 3) short passage based on knowledge of word meanings.

b. *Comprehension of Sequences*: matching of scrambled elements in a dialogue and completion of résumé of events described in the dialogue; sequencing of scrambled groups of four sentences.

c. *Retention of significant details*: unaided recall of material, by sentence-completion format.

d. *Use of Context*: sentence-completion in which context has to be used to choose a simple synonym for less familiar target words.

e. *Reading Rate*: a story with gaps in has to be read under strictly timed conditions (in fact all the sections have time limits). The appropriate word from sets of three has to be chosen to fill the gap and maintain continuity.

The sub-tests are used to comprise a five- 'stalk' profile to give a comparative picture of performance. The sub-tests are reported as being substantially intercorrelated although e) (Rate) is consistently less highly correlated with the other sub-tests.

A printed sheet is provided for recording group of individual profiles, and guidance is given for determining whether discrepancies are sufficiently great to imply differences of any substance. In addition a full description of the rationale of the sub-tests is given with

---

1   Sheet TIS 4501.

particularly helpful advice on the interpretation of unusually high or low scores. The manual commendably warns that the statistical characteristics of the test show a unitary dimension of reading is being tested but that for teaching purposes examination of individual differences in sub-tests can be useful, particularly for remedial work.

The test is certainly more demanding in its administrative requirements than most attainment tests. This difficulty illustrates the moral that richer and more sophisticated assessment of reading often necessitates more time and trouble than that involved with the simple group tests which teachers find most convenient to use.

Edinburgh Reading Tests Stage 3 intended for ages 10:0 to 12:6 ULP

Although constructed by Moray House College of Education Stage 3 is in principle very similar to Stage 2. Again five sections are employed:

a. *Reading for Facts*: statements about short prose passages must be endorsed as 'true', 'false' or 'doesn't say'.

b. *Comprehension of Sequences*: scrambled sentences have to be re-arranged in the correct order.

c. *Retention of Main Ideas*: unaided recall of short passages using multiple-choice completion of sentences in a résumé of the test passage.

d. *Comprehension of Point of View*: pupils read accounts of dialogues in which a number of characters' opinions are represented. A series of statements related to the topic discussed then have to be correctly attributed to the most likely character.

e. *Vocabulary*: sentence-completion and matching tasks similar to those in Stage 2.

Many of the comments about Stage 2 would apply to Stage 3. The tests attempt a sophistication and thoroughness that may be taken as either unrealistic or commendable, depending upon one's point of view. It seems likely that the test would satisfy teachers with a more ambitious and comprehensive conception of reading. However the test would seem to be far more complex and time-consuming than is necessary for the identification or assessment of the less able. On the other hand it should prove admirable as a means of assessing the competence of average and above average pupils on entry to secondary schools.

GAP Reading Comprehension Test
J. McLeod (UK Version by D. Unwin), Heinemann

The test has two equivalent forms containing seven and eight 'Cloze' passages of graded difficulty. The passages were selected for their capacity to elicit unequivocal response patterns from the original Australian children for whom the test was intended.

The manual briefly outlines the rationale of the cloze technique as a method of assessment and earlier work on the subject is mentioned. In addition, correlations of the GAP with conventional reading tests are presented. The test has the merit of being based upon some coherent *theory* of reading and provides a useful unitary measure of reading attainment.

The GAP versions appear to have succeeded in minimizing the writing/spelling load and the problems of multiplicity of acceptable responses associated with cloze testing, but the potential of the technique for assessment has still to be fully explored. The cloze technique is perhaps more theoretically justified than other test techniques and appears to test varied aspects of comprehension, ranging from use of context and understanding of language structure to the overall linguistic resources of the reader. It has yet to be shown, however, what practical advantages come with this theoretical superiority.

GAPADOL Reading Comprehension Test
J. McLeod and J. Anderson, Heinemann

Like the GAP test, the GAPADOL is a set of cloze test passages. It is intended for a higher age and ability group than that covered in the GAP test. Reading ages are given for pupils from 7:5 up to almost 17 years. These norms appear to be based on the original Australian sample however. It is inevitable that in such a wide range test only a few points of raw scores will separate widely different age groups. For example, the average pupil of 16:11 scores only four more points than the average pupil of 15:11. A table is included to indicate whether a pupil is retarded, normal or superior for his age. A retarded score places a pupil in the bottom 10 per cent of his age group. This table is particularly instructive as it shows a gradual widening of the gap between normal and retarded pupils and simultaneous narrowing of that between normal and superior readers.

Basically this means the efficiency of the test for the detection of backwardness increases with age, and its efficiency as an index of superiority decreases. This technique is however a consistent one, whereas the reading age scale is not. The retardation score always places a child in the bottom 10 per cent, whereas the criterion of '18 months backwardness' would apply to an increasingly large portion of pupils. For example, if a pupil was '18 months backward at 11 years he would be placed well and truly in the bottom 10 per cent of his age group. By contrast a '16-year-old who was 18 months backward would be well above the bottom 10 per cent of his age group. Further, a 16-year-old who was 18 months backward would have a raw score within five points of that which was 'normal' for 16-year-olds!

The harder test passages themselves are chosen from texts likely to be of interest to older secondary pupils and, unlike the GAP test, the answer words are written on a separate page in special boxes provided.

Although a question remains about the relevance of the norms the test is one which should be of interest to teachers in secondary schools.

Gates-MacGinitie Reading Tests (British Edition)
Primary A, Form 1. Vocabulary and Comprehension
A.I. Gates and W.H. MacGinitie (British Standardization by P. Saville and S. Blinkhorn), NFER Publishing Company

The vocabulary section of the test consists of a series of word-picture matching tasks; the more difficult items employ more complex and visually similar words. The Comprehension section requires the choice of the most appropriate illustration to go with the accompanying sentence or short paragraph.

The American flavour of the original test has been reduced by the modification of some of the items, and the highly pictorial nature of the test makes it particularly suitable for the less able reader. The standardization tables also make much finer distinctions between below average scores than between those over 100, a useful feature in a test intended for younger pupils as it aids early detection of those who are falling behind. The American technical report gives the correlation between the two parts as moderate rather than high at .67. Scores for both parts are also substantially correlated with Verbal IQ at the higher US grade levels. The report also gives extensive advice and information for evaluating differences between part scores and equivalent forms. It is a pity this is largely inapplicable to the British version.

In comparison to other seven-plus tests the Gates-MacGinitie is probably under-used in view of its merits. The Vocabulary section, with its emphasis on recognition of the meaning of words as opposed to merely being able to sound them, is of particular value as an additional test of word recognition which checks the validity of oral reading tests.

Group Reading Assessment
F.A. Spooncer, ULP

In Part 1 the pupils have to identify, from a printed set of five, the word spoken by the administrator. Part 2 is a simple sentence-completion test, while Part 3 involves identifying from a set of five the homophone of the target word.

The RAs for this test are in fact predicted scores on the Vernon *Graded Word Reading Test*. The Spooncer test was calibrated against the earlier norms for the Vernon test, although these were found to be too lenient. The standardized score tables provide more recent norms and the differences between the two possible interpretations of a pupil's performance need to be noted. The correlations with other reading tests are taken to substantiate the validity of the test.

Group Reading Test
D. Young, ULP

The test has two sections: word and picture matching, and sentence-completion in the form of choosing the correct synonym to match a stem. The easiest items were based partly on the vocabulary lists of Edwards and Gibbon's *Words Your Children Use*. The constructor has taken considerable care to validate the test against scores on other reading tests, and the final tables were calibrated on tests with nationally based norms. The differences between the two forms and the effect of practice are explained, and the manual gives sound general guidance about the limitations of testing and the interpretation of scores. The test has enjoyed popularity as an instrument for local authority surveys as well as for classroom use. The wide age-range of norms of the test are perhaps misleading. The conversion tables show the test is most effective for general use between 7:0 years and 7:11 only. It would be of use only for advanced readers below this level, or retarded readers above it.

The Holborn Reading Scale
A.F. Watts, Harrap

The scale is based on 33 short sentences for oral reading. The successful reading of each sentence earns the reader another three months of reading age, starting from a base of 5:9. A series of comprehension questions is included, but no norms are given for these questions. The easier questions are intended for oral administration; the more difficult ones use a multiple-choice format and the answer choices are to be written on the board so that this part of the test can be group-administered. As a test of mechanical reading — checked with comprehension — the scale does have the advantage of brevity;

however, the language ('the musician whose violin was interfered with has our sincere sympathy') is somewhat artificial and the norms are hopelessly out of date. In addition the norms provided seem to extend very much too far beyond the age range actually tested in standardization. The test is in wide use, although at the time of writing it is out of print.

The Kingston Test of Silent Reading
M.E. Hebron, Harrap

A single prose passage is used in which 52 of the words have been deleted at various intervals. The appropriate missing words have to be written on a separate piece of paper. In some cases alternative answers are permitted. The test is presented as a test of comprehension. Although the technique is similar to the cloze task it seems likely that the constructor was not directly using this as his underlying theory. However the test must enjoy many of the claims to validity made for cloze testing. Correlations with a number of reading and intelligence tests (mostly now out of print) are low to moderate. The newspaper column layout of the passage might prove confusing to some pupils and is probably an unfortunate printing economy rather than a controlled manipulation of the legibility of the passage.

The date of the norms — probably based upon a regional sample — raises a question about the contemporary value. It should also be noted that the norms are only appropriate for the more able readers below 8:6 and the less able above 10:6.

NFER Reading Test A
NFER Guidance and Assessment Service, NFER Publishing Co.

The test is made up entirely of sentence-completion items; in some cases a phrase has to be supplied from the set of four possibilities, rather than a word. The earlier items are printed in larger type.

The test has the advantage of recency of standardization in comparison to most other tests for children of seven-plus although the pattern of standardized scores at eight-plus suggest the test is more suitable for the less able at this level.

NFER Reading Test AD
A.F. Watts, NFER Publishing Co.

The sentence-completion task is again employed. In this case a word has to be chosen from a set of five to sensibly complete the sentence.

The test was formerly known as 'Sentence Reading Test 1' and has been widely used in research as well as by schools and local authorities. It has the advantage of covering a wide age-span, although where it is suspected a wide ability range exists in a seven-plus group an easier test would perhaps be preferable. The instructions direct that responses should be recorded on the test sheets, and this is a distinct economic disadvantage, as it is with many NFER tests.

NFER Reading Test BD
NFER Guidance and Assessment Service, NFER Publishing Co.

This test also uses a sentence-completion format. For the most part it is the final word in the sentence that has to be chosen. The test was formerly known as 'Sentence Reading Test 2'. Like Reading Test AD it has been used for research as well as educational purposes. Although the test has a wide age-span it will be on the hard side for pupils below eight years six months. Larger type is used for the first two pages, but even so the items are somewhat crowded onto the page; the less able may find this a somewhat overwhelming prospect.

NFER Reading Comprehension Test DE
E.L. Barnard, NFER Publishing Co.

Seven prose passages and a verse passage are employed. Each passage is accompanied by a number of questions, all of a multiple-choice or objectively marked variety. The provisional manual keys the questions as dealing with either 'global understanding', 'ability to draw conclusions', 'understanding of individual words and phrases', and 'ability to read for detail'. No research evidence is available to show the questions do really test these separate areas of comprehension. The test is very clearly presented, and is one of the few tests for junior-aged pupils which uses the prose comprehension method. The passages themselves are of a reasonable literary standard. The test would seem to have potential as a screening test for pupils entering some secondary schools as it would be more easily tackled by the less able 11- to 12-year-olds than some other tests standardized for this age group.

NFER Secondary Reading Test EH1: Vocabulary
S.M. Bate, NFER Publishing Co.

The test uses a sentence-completion format; the spaces occur both in the body of sentences and at their ends, and the level of vocabulary involved becomes rapidly more sophisticated.

Although norms are given for the first-year secondary age-range the test often proves difficult for the less able readers at this level. Even the early items are fairly hard and would prove equally difficult to the weak and very weak reader. As a result the test does not discriminate *within* backward groups.

Although the test is far from ideal for lower secondary pupils it is one of the few published tests which possess norms appropriate at this age level. No evidence is available to show how far 'Vocabulary' in this context is separate from 'Comprehension' (EH2) or 'Speed' (EH3).

NFER Secondary Reading Test EH2: Comprehension
S.M. Bate, NFER Publishing Co.

A series of comprehension passages — all from literary sources — with multiple-choice questions used.

The comments about difficulty for younger and less able pupils made for EH1 apply even more to this test. However it is again one of the few tests suitable at this age level in general. Although it is a demanding test the use of continuous prose in units longer than a sentence makes for a more valid task than those based on single sentences in that it is closer to the demands of everyday life and of school work.

NFER Secondary Reading Test EH3: Continuous Prose (Speed)
S.M. Bate, NFER Publishing Co.

The test is essentially one of rate of reading. Two continuous prose passages have to be read silently under strictly timed conditions. A check on comprehension is provided by the use of easy sentence-completion tasks throughout the passages. Raw scores are based on the number of correct completions. The test is thus one of rate of comprehension rather than sheer mechanical speed. The test often proves more difficult than EH1 and 2. This aspect of reading is rarely taught in British secondary schools although as a skill it would seem to have some pragmatic value. In this test no score is computed for the number of words correctly underlined in the test. The assumption is made that any pupil for whom the test was appropriate would only underline a 'wrong' word, accidentally. Although the provisional manual for the test does not say so, it would be meaningless to give a score for any pupil who did not manage to choose the right words for most of his answers. The test is concerned with how quickly a pupil can read and this presupposes that he can already read fairly well in unpaced situations.

Progressive Achievement Tests: Reading Comprehension and Vocabulary
W.B. Elley and N.A. Reid, ULP

The New Zealand Council for Educational Research produced these tests in 1969 and the percentile norms provided are for New Zealand children between eight and 14 years.

The publishers recommend the tests are used in the UK for their criterion-referenced characteristics. These were developed in the course of research into readability and vocabulary counts, and take the form of comprehension and vocabulary 'level' scores.

A pupil's vocabulary score can thus be used to indicate the size and scope of his reading vocabulary. For example, a pupil with a raw vocabulary score of 18 is at level four. This means he has a vocabulary of 'up to 4000 words' and probably knows the meaning of between 3000 and 4000 of the most commonly used 10,000 words.

The comprehension test gives a level score which corresponds to the level of 'readability' of prose material a pupil can comprehend. Examples of material at each of the levels are mentioned in the manual. Most of these would be more familar to New Zealand teachers than to those in Britain. Supplementary instructions are included to enable a teacher to estimate the readability of any materials not mentioned.

The principle is a promising one in that test scores are supposed to measure what the teacher can expect the child to actually do. Unlike many criterion-referenced tests, the *Progressive Achievement Tests* have some research behind them to show they are measuring the criteria under consideration. The instructions claim that the 'noun-frequency' count method used to measure readability is accurate. However the method has yet to be evaluated independently and it is a notorious feature of readability research that independent studies of such techniques do not agree upon their validity. Elley's research evidence is probably sufficiently strong to justify the use of the tests is an experimental spirit.

In format the tests break no new ground. The vocabulary tests are of the sentence-completion variety, and comprehension is tested by prose passages followed by objective multiple-choice questions. The norms suggest the tests are most suitable for the upper junior and lower secondary age-range.

Reading and Spelling Tests (R1, R2, R3, R4, S1, S2)
F.J. Schonell, Oliver and Boyd

R1 (Schonell Graded Word Reading Test) is a graded word recognition test consisting of ten words, each of which is to be read orally. Each word read constitutes 0.1 of a year in reading age. For many teachers this has been *the* reading test and is still in wider use than any other British reading test.

R2 (Simple Prose Reading Test) is an oral reading and recall test. A simple five-paragraph story is read orally; then 15 questions about the passage have to be answered from memory. Scores are based upon accuracy and speed of reading and comprehension.

R3 (Silent Reading Test A) is a series of short paragraphs, each of which is followed by a single comprehension question.

R4 (Silent Reading Test B) is a sentence-completion test. Each item consists of a paragraph in which two words have to be supplied from two sets of five. The test differs from single sentence-completion items in that the sentences occur in the context of increasingly longer paragraphs.

S1 and S2 (Graded Word Spelling Tests A and B) consist of lists of words which are dictated in a context devised by the teachers. Each correctly spelt word earns 0.1 of a year in spelling age.

For the main part the norms for the Schonell tests are distinctly dated and no information seems to be available on the original standardization. However, in the case of the Graded Word Reading Test some useful norms for a restandardization with Cheshire children are available from the NFER Publishing Company (Test Information Sheet 4501). It is perhaps unfortunate that the other tests which are in many ways superior in content do not have similar norms. The Silent Reading Tests A and B in particular equal in excellence of content tests produced more recently. Many of the objections to the Word Recognition test would be less urgent if only it was used as part of the complete Schonell battery instead of isolation.

Richmond Tests of Basic Skills
A.N. Hieronymns and E.F. Lindquist, Nelson

These tests are a British version of an established American test battery, the *Iowa Tests of Basic Skills*. Two tests in the battery deal directly with reading: Vocabulary and Comprehension.

Both use a multiple-choice format. The Vocabulary Tests are limited to synonym-type questions:

Close the door
a) shut (correct answer)
b) hold
c) behind
d) open

Comprehension consists entirely of a series of prose passages followed by objective multiple-choice questions. The tests have been prepared to meet six levels of difficulty, appropriate for successive age groups between 8:1 and 14:0 years.

Each year group starts and finishes at points increasingly further on in the test. Thus the first level of the Vocabulary test covers items one to 31, the second level items 11 to 48, and so on.

An attempt has been made to classify items in the comprehension test under four main skills:

1. *Details*: recognition and understanding of stated or implied factual details and relationships.
2. *Purpose*: skill in discerning the purpose or main idea in the text.
3. *Organization*: ability to organize ideas.
4. *Evaluation*: skill in evaluating what is read.

Further sub-skills are described within each skill area, but the manual points out that *all* items in the test were too highly correlated for the use of a separate score for each skill to be justified.

The manual contains a number of suggestions on the diagnostic use of the tests and possible remedial activities. It also makes some judicious remarks on the way tests should reflect the objectives of teaching and the relative importance to be attached to different test items and their related objectives.

Technically the tests appear to have been competently developed for use in Britain. Standardization was carried out on a sample of 17,000 children, and normative scores are provided in the form of percentiles and standardized scores, with an age-adjustment. There is unfortunately no information on reliability and validity studies.

The tests are printed in re-usable booklets which include other tests in the battery of mathematics, work study skills and language skills of spelling, punctuation and use of capitals. Diagnostic classification schemes and norms are also provided for these tests. The tests provide an extremely convenient and comprehensive package of assessment materials — machine marking is in fact possible.

There is perhaps a danger that they will be used in an unthinking and automatic routine. While they are outstandingly convenient to use the actual content of the tests is perhaps restricted.

Southgate Group Reading Test: Test 1, Word Selection Test
V. Southgate, ULP

   The test task involves detection of words spoken by the tester from printed sets of five. In some cases a picture of the target word is provided.

   The test is intended for use with younger children than group reading tests commonly cater for. It is also appropriate for less able older pupils who are still having problems with word-recognition. High correlations with both teachers' ratings and individual word and sentence reading tests are reported.

   It is suggested the test is appropriate for much older pupils who obtain low scores on more difficult tests. This is certainly a useful function — the problem of assessing less able readers with tests only generally appropriate to their age group has already been stressed. With such children the reading age value may be useful: two 14-year-olds who both obtain standardized scores of 70 on a harder test may have markedly different reading ages on this test. However, the limitations of the norms must be considered: they are now a little out of date and originally were based upon a single population of children in one urban local authority.

Southgate Group Reading Tests: Test 2 — Sentence-Completion Test
V. Southgate, ULP

   A simple sentence-completion exercise is used throughout. In each case a single word has to be chosen from a set of five to sensibly end the sentence. The test is intended as an extension to Test 1 and can be used in the middle junior years. It is also recommended for the more advanced infant children and slower top junior and secondary children. Tests 1 and 2 can be used in conjunction when a wide range of attainment is suspected to exist amongst the group to be tested.

   The validity of the test is based on high correlations with the Schonell Graded Word Reading Test and NFER Reading Test AD.

   The user of this test should study the notes and tables relating to the norms given on pages 19—22 of the manual. The distributions of raw scores are highly skewed and do not reflect the normal curve upon which interpretation of test scores is usually based. The histograms show that between eight years nine months and eight years 11 months the test stratifies the less able readers very effectively but does not discriminate between average and advanced readers. Between seven years nine months and seven years 11 months relatively few pupils obtain the 'expected' reading age of seven years 10 months and the test allocates the majority of pupils to either a distinctly advanced group (RAs in the region of nine years) or a distinctly backward group (RAs of seven years or less).

This means that reading ages would have widely different relative meanings at different chronological ages. An informed user could employ the variable characteristics of the test to positive purpose. A less informed user would be in danger of being misled by the test results. The main point is that the Southgate test covers two early stages of learning to read and once a level of 9:6 is reached a child is beyond the scope of the tests.

Vernon Graded Word Reading Test
P.E.,Vernon, ULP

When re-standardizing the Burt test in 1938 P.E. Vernon produced his own word-recognition test. The original norms for Scottish children have only the most limited value today. When a GWRT is required at all the Schonell and Burt (Rearranged) tests would seem to have more relevant norms available.

Wide-Span Reading Test
A. Brimer and H. Gross, Nelson

The test uses a somewhat unusual sentence-completion format. The answer word has to be supplied from a second clue-giving sentence on the left of the problem sentence.

Individual performances can be analysed diagnostically by inspection of the pattern of errors that are made. These can be classified as due to Decoding, Linguistic or Vocabulary weaknesses, depending upon which wrong word the child picks out of the clue-sentence.

The scoring systems available with this test are very sophisticated and the diagnostic facility appears promising, although no data about its validity are presented. The potential breadth of the age range covered by the test is impressive, although the language of the later items is deliberately made tortuous and artifical. The test may prove somewhat formidable for the less able and younger readers in view of its overall length and the density of the first page.

The novel method of testing raises considerable problems also. Although it may have diagnostic possibilities its validity as a test of reading attainment is questionable for two reasons:

1) The deliberate use of artificial language means the reader is being

tested on content which is unfamiliar and remote from the reading material upon which he will have been practising and developing his skill.

2) The two sentences are unrelated in meaning, for example:

The passengers waited patiently   Fishing is a sport which
for the train   requires both skill and _____
                                              (not from original Text)

The exercise is thus one which appears to require inductive and verbal reasoning skills unrelated to processes normally involved in reading, while actively discouraging the thought processes of context-use involved in real reading. Some linguistic and semantic knowledge is of course required to complete the test-sentence with the word 'patience'. For example the testee must appreciate that a noun is required, none of the nouns in the cue sentence are semantically appropriate, but that a transform of the adverb 'patiently' would fit. Yet these processes are equally well-tested by traditional sentence-completion tasks, or by cloze tests.

On the other hand, the re-usable test booklets give the test a distinct practical advantage over many of these tests.

Diagnostic tests

Domain Phonic Test and Phonic Workshop
J. McLeod and J. Atkinson, Oliver and Boyd

Four word recognition tests similar in appearance to the conventional Graded Word Recognition are provided. The words are chosen systematically to present a comprehensive selection of vowel-consonant combinations and blends in various configurations. The pupil's oral errors are recorded and the pattern of errors is plotted on a grid which indicates which of the 63 exercises in the attached Phonic Workshop would be appropriate.

Test P1: Beginning and ending consonants and vowels in three-letter words.

Test P2: Single initial consonants followed by vowel blends.

Test P3: Single vowels with beginning or ending consonant blends.

Test P4: Vowel blends and consonant blends combined in single words.

Test P5: A supplementary auditory discrimination test in which pairs of common words are spoken by the tester. Nine of these are identical, the remaining 41 differ only in one phoneme. The test is intended to identify inability to discriminate between sounds within words.

Full guidance in the recording and interpretation of errors and many of the phonic units are repeated so that specific difficulties can be identified with reliability. The remedial materials included are systematic in their coverage although most teachers would want to expand upon them considerably. The value of the test lies in the thoroughness with which phonic knowledge is covered; there would be little chance that even highly specific difficulties would be overlooked.

Doren Diagnostic Reading Test of Word Recognition Skills
M. Doren, Nelsons

This is a group test of word recognition skills which is produced in America but is now available in the UK. The test covers 12 main skill areas and reflects a 'whole-word' approach rather than an exclusively phonic approach. The test is divided up as follows:

1. Letter Recognition
2. Beginning Sounds
3. Whole Word Recognition
4. Words within Words
5. Speech Consonants
6. Ending Sounds
7. Blending
8. Rhyming
9. Vowels
10. Discriminate Guessing
11. Spelling
12. Sight Words

Most of the skill areas are subdivided further so the test provides an outstandingly comprehensive coverage of word recognition skills. A range of testing techniques are employed, although essentially most of them involve a multiple-choice format. The test places emphasis upon the ability to match and discriminate and use context. Even the items with a phonic emphasis include contextual cues. For example, the Consonant Blend sub-test of Skill 7 'measures the ability to apply known blends to independent word selection in context'. These items thus involve a sentence-frame which has to be completed as in the following example:

fled
flag
flat   When they saw the _____ the soldiers _____ from
float   the wall of the castle.

                                            (not from the test)

It is possible to record either group or individual scores in a 12-point profile and the manual contains both advice on remedial teaching — mainly of the whole-word type — and some information about validity.

As many teachers prefer to use a mixture of phonic and other word-recognition skills in their teaching the Doren test might prove to be a useful accompaniment to other exclusively phonic tests, such as the Swansea and Carver tests.

Get Reading Right (Phonic Skills Test)
S. Jackson, Gibson of Glasgow

The phonic skills tests are accompanied by a handbook for remedial teaching ranging from pre-reading skills to the level of attainment typical of nine- and 10-year-olds. The tests are largely concerned with phonic knowledge and the accompanying manual gives advice on remediation in both word analysis and overall strategies of word-attack. The first test is a group-screening instrument and the remainder are a series of individual oral word-reading tests for which the tester records any errors.

Tests 1 & 2:	Group Tests of letter-recognition
Tests 3 & 4:	Individual tests of letter-recognition
Test 5:	Simple two and three-letter words
Test 6:	Final consonant blends
Test 7:	Initial consonant blends
Test 8:	Vowel digraphs
Test 9:	Consonant digraphs
Test 10:	Word-endings
Test 11:	Multi-syllable words

The tests and the exercises in the handbook give a thoroughly structured — although flexible — approach to the teaching of phonic skills. Less attention is given to the very fundamental perceptual difficulties which might show up on the *Standard Reading Tests*, and peripheral areas such as spelling and copying are ignored in favour of a more intensive coverage of decoding skills. The absence of statistical data is of little importance in a test of this kind. Instead the scheme provides an effective and viable remedial programme, particularly for teachers with little prior experience of remedial work. Like the *Domain* test, *Get Reading Right* is a very systematic phonic test, although it probably takes longer to administer in its entirety.

Harrison-Stroud Reading Readiness Profiles
M.L. Harrison and J.B. Stroud, NFER Publishing Co.

The 'profiles' are based on six sub-tests for measuring eight 'readiness skills'. The scores are used to portray a six-point profile of the child's readiness skills.

Test 1:   *Using Symbols:* Printed words have to be matched with the appropriate pictures. In each case a fair copy of the target word and picture match is provided. It is therefore unnecessary for the child to be able to decode the words.

Test 2:   *Making Visual Discriminations*: In 2a the identical form of the target word has to be chosen from sets of visually similar words. In 2b pupils perform the task with less directive support from the teacher, so that capacity for independent working and attention span may be examined.

Test 3:   *Using the Context*: A picture of an object referred to indirectly in a short story read by the tester has to be chosen from a set of three.

Test 4:   *Making Auditory Discrimination*: Pictures whose words have the same initial sound have to be matched.

Test 5:   *Using Context and Auditory Clues*: A combined version of the tasks in tests 3 and 4 is employed. Both oral context and auditory clues have to be used to identify the correct picture.

Test 6:   *Giving the Names of the Letters*: This is an individual test in which the pupil has to name upper and lower case letters printed on a card.

The authors claim that the test tasks are 'intrinsically valid' as they test readiness skills directly. No other validity data are presented and this claim is really not adequate to justify the use of the test on an extensive basis, although the test profiles are in areas generally thought to be important in the development of reading skill. The profiles may thus be useful when applied selectively to individual cases and interpreted sensibly.

Developmental Tests of Visual Perception
Marianne Frostig, NFER Publishing Co.

A diagnosis of perceptual retardation is made on the basis of five pencil-and-paper tests of perceptual development:

a. *Eye-Motor Coordination*: drawing lines between points, with and without boundaries.
b. *Figure-Ground*: individual geometrical shapes have to be identified from within increasingly complex background configurations.
c. *Constancy of Shape*: geometrical target shapes have to be identified under varying conditions of size, context and orientation.
d. *Position in Space*: a visual discrimination test in which inverted or reversed members of identical sets must be detected (Similar to Test 4 of Daniels and Diack's *Standard Reading Tests*).
e. *Spatial Relationships*: line patterns have to be copied using dots as a framework.

The tests attempt to anticipate perceptual problems that may be encountered if the pupil is introduced to printed language prematurely. The five areas chosen reflect the author's clinical experience, and studies are cited to support the theory that these are independent. The test has proven a moderately effective predictor of early reading progress amongst samples of American children.

The test can be given in modified form to deaf children — in normal form the verbal instructions are substantial — and a remedial training kit is available — although this is probably too expensive for use by most infant schools.

Little is known about the pattern of usage of the test in Britain although it is probably used more by educational psychologists than teachers. The number of children for whom such a test would be appropriate is probably fairly small; pupils who manifest marked difficulty on sub-tests 2, 3 and 4 of the *Standard Reading Tests* might benefit from further analysis with the Frostig test.

The Neale Analysis of Reading Ability
M.D. Neale, Macmillan

The test consists of six graded oral reading passages. These are used to assess simple comprehension, rate of reading and the pattern of errors. These are classified as:

Mispronounciations

Substitutions
Refusals
Additions
Omissions
Reversals

The number of correct words is used to give an accuracy score.

Three supplementary tests of letter (lower and upper case) names and sounds, spelling and auditory discrimination, and blending and syllable-recognition are included.

Evidence for validity is based on correlations with other reading tests. Some mention is also made of the statistical validity for the three separate score scales. The Neale test is widely used in Britain and is based on the format used by many well-established American tests. It takes oral reading behaviour — particularly error patterns — as the means of examining a reader's problem. It has the advantage of assessing reading in context but focuses mainly on the mechanical aspects of reading; success at the comprehension tasks appears to be largely a matter of memory of the content of the test passages.

The depth of diagnosis is relatively modest, the test appears mainly to deal with word-attack. The scores yield more hard information about attainment and in this respect the test-norms maybe somewhat dated. A more elaborate but generally similar American prototype of the Neale, the *Durrell Analysis of Reading Difficulty* is in fact available in Britain from the NFER Publishing Company. This test is very much more expensive, and seems to provide very little more information than the Neale.

NFER Tests of Proficiency in English
NFER, NFER Publishing Co.

The tests are primarily intended for the assessment of linguistic competence in non-native speakers of English in the early years of schooling. They make extensive use of pictorial material (half the characters portrayed are clearly immigrant types such as Asian and West-Indian), and the material reflects three levels of skill and development.

Listening:
Level 1: identification of pictures appropriate to short statements read aloud by the tester.
Level 2: identification of pictures matching oral (tape-recorded) information.

Level 3: multiple-choice comprehension of short passages (both passages and questions are tape-recorded).

Reading:
Levels 1 & 2: matching pictures with printed statements.
Level 3: Multiple-choice comprehension of short printed passages.

Speaking:
Level 1: pupil has to name activities portrayed by pictures.
Level 2: pupil has to name activities in more elaborate sentence form and supply contextually appropriate versions of what characters are saying at the end of simple pictorially portrayed narrative episodes.
Level 3: pupil has to continue utterances from a stem supplied by the tester ('Before he . . .'; 'As soon as . . .' etc.) and describe pictorial episodes and continue the narrative by saying what he thinks happens next.
For the Speaking tests all the pupil's responses are tape recorded.

Writing:
Level 1: pupil has to give written descriptions of pictured objects and activities.
Level 2: more elaborate picture-description and completion of printed sentences.
Level 3: completion of sentences requiring longer responses and continuous writing on one of three essay titles.

The tests include a certain amount of shared material in the four skill areas, so that differentials in levels of attainment can be studied across skills. Pupils' performance in speaking and writing is scored in terms of a scale of Intelligibility and linguistic units called T-units. A T-unit is defined as 'one main clause plus any subordinate clauses related to it'.

Pupils are classified into three levels which correspond to their level of linguistic competence and general instructional needs. Further diagnostic analysis can be made by close study of the very full grammatical breakdown of the test material described in the *General Guide*.

The tests enable a complex qualitative analysis of pupils' linguistic development to be made. This however requires an energetic and informed attitude on the part of the teacher. While the linguistic information indicates much about the material and content of remedial teaching, no evidence is produced to show how exactly teachers might act on it, and the model of language behind the tests is a rather naive one, for example, the assumption is made that spoken and written forms of language are identical. The tests seem to have found favour as a means of assessing immigrant pupils on entry to the British education system — i.e. screening. This is rather different from genuine diagnosis however. The psycholinguistic reality of the three levels is itself open to question and one may question the validity of the arbitarily set raw scores used as criteria to place children at a particular level.

Standard Reading Tests
J.C. Daniels and H. Diack, Chatto and Windus

Test 1: *The Standard Test of Reading Skill* A series of printed sentences has to be read aloud. The order of difficulty of the words reflects order of phonic difficulty; scores thus express both attainment and development of phonic knowledge.

Test 2: *Copying Abstract Figures* Four abstract designs have to be copied. Pupils' efforts are appraised for accuracy and 'neatness'. The tasks are used to assess perceptual discrimination and organization and motor coordination.

Test 3: *Copying a Sentence* A single sentence has to be copied — neatness and spacing of words are basis of assessment.

Test 4: *Visual Discrimination and Orientation Test* Pictures, patterns, letter combinations and words have to be matched with identical forms from sets of four possible matches — only one of which will be identical. Confusion over mirror images and left-right orientation are investigated by this test.

Test 5: *Letter-Recognition Test* The names or sounds of isolated letters have to be supplied by the pupil. Alternatively he can be asked to indicate initial or end letters of words spoken by the tester. The test is recommended as a means of determining readiness for instruction in phonics.

Test 6: *Aural Discrimination* Auditory analysis is tested by identification of pictures on the basis of the initial sound of their words. A success rate of at least nine out of 12 correct is considered necessary for success in learning to read, and guidance is given on the possibility of detecting certain forms of deafness.

Test 7: *Diagnostic Word-Recognition Tests* Simple word recognition tasks are used to test eight aspects of phonics:

a) Phonically simple two-and three-letter words
b) Initial consonant blends
c) Terminal consonant blends

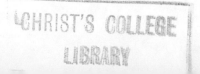

  d) Polysyllabic words
  e) Graded phonically complex words
  f) Reversible words
  g) Nonsense words

Test 8: *Oral Word-Recognition* The printed forms of words spoken by the tester have to be identified as a test of various aspects of word-analysis.

Test 9: *Picture Word-Recognition Test* Words have to be chosen to match pictures appropriately. The words are sufficiently similar to provide a test of silent auditory analysis.

Test 10: *Silent Prose-Reading and Comprehension* The pupil reads a passage to himself and then reads aloud, and answers a number of questions without referring back to the story. The test is intended as a check that mechanical reading does not occur without a comparable degree of comprehension, but no norms are provided.

Test 11: *Graded Spelling Test* The pupils have to spell words spoken by the tester. Age norms are provided, together with some guidance for the analysis of errors.

Test 12: *Graded Test of Reading Experience* A 50-item sentence-completion test. Age norms are provided although the unreliability of scores above 10:0 is stressed. The test is intended as a further check on the comprehension level of the reader.

The *Standard Reading Tests* are widely used by both psychologists and teachers. Although individual users sometimes express dissatisfaction with particular sub-tests the general usefulness of the tests with retarded readers is undisputed. The authors do not provide details about standardization reliability and validity, and although the excellence of the content partly compensates for this their normative value is limited.

Swansea Test of Phonic Skills
P. Williams, Blackwell

The test attempts to assess phonic knowledge by presenting phonic units in the form of nonsense words. This approach enables assessment of phonic elements without confounding effects due to a sight vocabulary of semantic context. The test consists of 65 items in the form of printed sets of five nonsense words. The word to be identified is that spoken by the tester.

The words in each set vary only in a single phonic element. The test task is thus one of discrimination in a particular phonic area, possibly leading to the identification of specific weaknesses. The following areas were chosen, on the basis of their frequency in early readers and word lists:

a) Short vowels
b) Long vowels
c) Initial letter blends
d) Final letter blends
e) Vowel combinations, initial and final consonant digraphs

A table is provided to indicate retardation in each of the five areas. An additional table indicates the order of difficulty in grapheme recognition displayed by infant pupils in the original experimental work. Reading ages are provided, being based on the correlation of the test with the Southgate Group Reading Test 1. The correlation with the Southgate test was .78 and this is perhaps low to be taken as a basis for equivalent reading ages.

The greatest value resides in the information about pupils' phonic knowledge. This however depends upon a thoughtful interpretation of results in the light of explanatory material in the manual and is only intended as a pointer for more intensive analysis. Further it must be recognized that phonics is only one aspect of word recognition and the artificial system of testing employed is not an example for teaching methods.

Thackray Reading Readiness Profiles
D. and L. Thackray, ULP

At present these profiles are the only tests of reading readiness developed and standardized on British children. The authors feel their test deals with skills which can be built up to aid success in learning to read. The profiles consist of three groups of tests and an adapted version of the Draw-a-Man Test.

Profile 1: *Vocabulary and Concept Development*: In this the child has to select a picture which goes with a word spoken by the teacher. The pictures represent objects and concepts likely to be within a young child's experience. The test is similar in principle to the *English Picture Vocabulary Test* described in Chapter 5.

Profile 2: *Auditory Discrimination*: This involves the matching of pictures of objects on the basis of the similarity of the initial phonemes of the words which name the objects.

Profile 3:   *Visual Discrimination*: In this test an identical match for a target word has to be selected from a set of four distractors. The child does not have to 'read' the words, but merely recognize visual similarities and differences.

Profile 4:   *General Ability:* The children are asked in this test to draw a picture of their 'Mummy'. This technique for the testing of intelligence and mental development is well-established and the interpretation of such drawings has been developed into a detailed scheme. However the Thackrays recommend a simple five point scale, A to E, based on the accuracy of the child's drawing. An 'E' rated drawing would be 'barely recognizable as human' while an 'A' rated figure should be moderately well-proportioned and generally anatomically accurate. Some additonal comments are made about the way such drawings may reflect children's emotional problems as well as lack of mental development.

The other three tests are also scores on an A to E scale, so that a child's performance on all four tests can be compared 'in profile'. In each case Level A contains the top seven per cent of children in the standardization sample, Level B the next 24 per cent and Level E the bottom seven per cent.

Intercorrelations for the profiles range from .31 to .52 and they are generally lower than the correlation of individual profiles with validity criteria such as the Schonell, Southgate and Neale reading tests which were administered to samples of children one year after the Thackray tests. The tests are thus moderately good predictors of reading success and are sufficiently independent of each other for the distinction between the four sub-tests to be worthwhile.

The tests have much in common with existing American readiness tests, such as the *Metropolitan Readiness Tests* and the *Harrison-Stroud Reading Readiness Profiles*. The fact that they draw upon established material and do not break new ground is not a criticism however. The strength of the tests lies in the use of established research and test development and in the efforts taken to validate and standardize the result. We have already remarked that the concept of readiness is a difficult one. Readiness and readiness testing are matters which teachers must approach thoughtfully and critically. There have certainly been some alarming cases of teachers who have completely misunderstood the purpose of limitations of readiness testing, possibly to the detriment of their pupils. Technically the tests are somewhat error prone. For example the standard error of Profile 3 is 2.5, which is almost as large as some of the level bands. One could therefore not safely label a child as an 'E' if he happened to score three on the test.

Word Recognition Test
C. Carver, ULP

The test task involves the identification of words spoken by the teacher from sets of five or six individual words. Some of the words are non-meaningful and the sets are devised to highlight separate or combined aural and visual errors in nine general classes of error:

a) Initial letters
b) Mid-vowel sounds
c) Distortions/twistings of letters
d) Distortions of words
e) Reversals
f) Word endings
g) Initial multiple consonants
h) Combined vowels
i) Regular (phonic) and irregular (sight) words

General guidance is given on how the pattern of the child's responses should be studied. Further interpretations can be made in the light of a table of general stages in word recognition and phonic knowledge.

The test offers a considerable advance over traditional methods of assessing word recognition in that it gives such full guidance on the qualitative assessment of reading. On the one hand the style of word recognition is observed, and on the other the general level of phonic knowledge is indicated. An additional asset is the full statistical validation which is reported.

The user is cautioned not to be over literal or mechanical in interpreting performance — although the general progression of reading development covered in the test is a useful guide. Like the Swansea test the Carver test is only a partial test of word recognition. This limitation apart, the test is one which teachers seem to have found particularly useful in practice.

Attainment tests

Title	Age Range	Sample Size	Approx. Date of Standard- ization	Equiv. Forms	Internal Consis- tency	Test Re-Test	SEm	Score System	Form	Time
Burt (Re-arranged) Word Recognition Tests (also known as the Burt-Vernon GWRT)	5:3 -16:8	Most recent norms for 6044 Cheshire children	1921 (1972)					RA	Indivi- dual	Untimed – a few minutes
Edinburgh Reading Tests. Stage 2	8:6 -10:6	2,764 Scotland 2,745 England & Wales	1971		.97		2.60	RA/SS	Group	1hr. 45m.
Edinburgh Reading Tests. Stage 3	10.0 -12:6	2,865 Scotland 2,793 England & Wales	1972		.97		2.60	RA/SS	Group	1hr. 50m.
GAP Reading Comprehension Test	7:5 -12:6+	1000+ England & Scotland	pre 1970	L & M		.83 .91	2.76	RA	Group	15 mins.
GAPADOL Reading Comprehension Test	up to 16:11	NA	1965	G/Y	.84-.93		3.47	RA+RS Scores	Group	30 mins.
Gates–MacGinitie Reading Tests Primary of Form 1 Vocabulary & Comprehension		4,768 England	1972	For US norms only	.97 .99	.95 .92	2.8 to 0.94 (raw score)	SS	Group	15 & 25 mins.
Group Reading Assessment (Spooncer)	7:8 -8:9	2,200 1st-year junior pupils	1963-4		.97	.96 .91	2.60 to 4.5	RA/SS	Group	16 mins.
Group Reading Test (Young)	6:6 -12:11	5,600 urban pupils		A/B		.95	see manual	RA/SS	Group	13 mins.

...ation Tests (cont.)

Title	Age Range	Sample Size	Approx. Date of Standard-ization	Equiv. Forms	Internal Consis-tency	Test Re-Test	SEm	Score System	Form	Time
Holborn Reading Scale	6:6 –11:0+	2,469 pupils in Infant & Junior Schools	pre-1944 (now out of print)					RA	Indivi-dual	
Kingston Test of Silent Reading	7:0 –10:11	2,000 rural & urban pupils (late in 2nd junior year)	pre-1954		.98		2.12	RA/SS	Group	20 mins.
NFER Reading Test A	6:9 –8:9	7,249 pupils from five LEA's	1971–72		.96		2.88	SS	Group	30 mins.
NFER Reading Test AD	7:6 –11:1	7,776 English	1955 Checked 1965		.94		3.6	SS	Group	15 mins.
NFER Reading Test BD	7:0 –10:4 (10:0 –11:4)	19,046 English	1969		.92		2.5	SS	Group	20 mins.
NFER Reading Comprehension Test DE	10:0 –11:9	5,538 W. Mid 1,687 E. Eng. 2,858 E. Eng.	1971 1971 1971		r values for later samples (1973) .94 and .93 (KR21) with SEm's of 3.7 and 3.9			SS	Group	40 mins.
NFER Reading Test EH1 Vocabulary	11:02 –12.05 Pro-visional norms for 12:06 –15:06	13,000 British children	1974		r values from .88 to .93 (KR21) with SEm's from 3.9 to 5.0 on subsequent samples			SS	Group	15–20 mins.

Attainment Tests (cont.)

Title	Age Range	Sample Size	Approx. Date of Standardization	Equiv. Forms	Internal Consistency	Test Re-Test	SEm	Score System	Form	Time
NFER Reading Test EH2 Comprehension	11:02 –12:06 Provisional norms for 12:06 –16:06	9,000 British children	1974		r values from .80 to .81 (KR21) with SEm's of 6.1 and 6.5 on subsequent samples			SS	Group	40–45 mins.
NFER Reading Test EH3 Continuous Prose	1st–4th year secondary Provisional norms for groups tested subsequently available	Approx. 1,000 per year group	1966		r of .77 and SEm of 7.1 for one sample			SS	Group	7 or 4½ mins.
Progressive Achievement Tests, Reading Vocabulary and Comprehension	8:0 –14:0	6,750 New Zealand	1968	A/B	.88–.94	.83–.91	2.4–3.6	Level scores & percentiles	Group	40 & 50 mins.
Richmond Test of Basic Skills, Tests V (vocabulary) and R (comprehension)	8:1 –14:0	1,700 British children	1974	Some re-testing possible				SS Stanines	Group	17 & 55 mins.
Schonell Reading and Spelling Tests: Graded Word Recognition Test R1	5:1 –16:8	Most recent norms for 6,321 Cheshire children	1950 1972					RA	Individual	Untimed – a few minutes

Attainment Tests (cont.)

Title	Age Range	Sample Size	Approx. Date of Standard-ization	Equiv. Forms	Internal Consis-tency	Test Re-Test	SEm	Score System	Form	Time
Simple Prose Reading Test R2	6:0 –9:5							RA	Indivi-dual	5 mins.
Silent Reading Test A R3	6:9 –12+							RA	Group	9 + mins.
Silent Reading Test B R4	6:9 –13+							RA	Group	15 mins.
Graded Word Spelling Tests S1/S2	5:1 –15:0			A/B				SA	Group	Untimed – 20 mins.
Southgate Group Reading Test 1: Word Selection Test	5:9 –8:1	2,329 pupils from an urban borough	1957	A/B/C		.96	1.38 to 2.10 raw score	RA	Group	20 mins.
Southgate Group Reading Test 2 Sentence-Completion Test	7:0 –10:11	3,751 pupils from an urban borough	1960	A/B		.97	1.76 to 2.89 raw score	RA	Group	15 mins.
Wide-span Reading Test	1st year junior 4th year second-ary	7,503 approx. 930 in each age group England and Wales	pre-1972	A/B		.89 to .95	3.5 to 5.0	SS	Group	30 mins.

Diagnostic tests

Title	Age Range	Sample Size	Approx. Date of Standard-ization	Equiv. Forms	Internal Consis-tency	Test Re-Test	SEm	Score System	Form	Time
Assessment of Reading Ability. (Phonic)	5:0 –9:9	145	1970						Indivi-dual	
Domain Phonic Test (Phonic)	Any age		1972						Indivi-dual	

Diagnostic Tests (cont.)

Title	Age Range	Sample Size	Approx. Date of Standard- ization	Equiv. Forms	Internal Consis- tency	Test Re-Test	SEm	Score System	Form	Time
Doren Diagnostic Test of Word Recognition Skills	Infant/ Junior		1956, 1973					raw score		Untimed
Get Reading Right (Phonic)	Any age		1971						Groups and Indivi- dual	
Harrison—Stroud Reading Readiness Profiles (Reading Readiness)	5:0 upwards	American 1st grade pupils	1955					Percen- tiles	Small Group and indi- vidual	80 mins.
Marianne Frostig Developmental Test of Visual Perception Perceptual	up to 10:0	2,100 American children from 3:0 to 9:0	1963		.78 to .89	.80		Percep- tual Ages Percent- iles and others	Group or indi- vidual	30—44 mins.
Neale Analysis of Reading Ability (Mechanical Reading)	6:0 –13+	2,000 from 13 English Schools	pre-1958	A/B/C		.92 .98		RA	Indivi- dual	10—15 mins.
NFER Tests of Proficiency in English. (Linguistic)	Infant & Junior	1,400 Asian & W. Indian children	1972—73		.63 to .85 for (some parts only)		1.6 to 2.3 (for some parts)	Level Scores	Groups & indi-	
Standard Reading Tests. (Diagnostic battery, perceptual and phonic)	5:2 –14+	No details published	pre-1958					RA	Groups & indi- vidual	

Diagnostic Tests (cont.)

Title	Age Range	Sample Size	Approx. Date of Standard- ization	Equiv. Forms	Internal Consis- tency	Test Re-Test	SEm	Score System	Form	Time
Swansea Test of Phonic Skills. (Phonic)	Pupils with RA's below 7:6		1969–70			.87 .93		RA	Group	40 mins.
Thackray Reading Readiness Profiles (Read, Readiness)	4:8 –5.8	5,500 children	1973			.80 –.90	2.1 –2.5	A–E scale	Group	70 mins.
Word Recognition Test Carver (Phonic)	up to 8:6	1,005 infant & lower juniors	pre-1970			.91 –.98		Word Recog- nition Age	Group	15–30 mins.

Appendices

APPENDIX A: Measurement of progress and the standard error.

Because the unreliability of standardized tests leads to a normal distribution of errors (see Chapter Three) it is possible to predict the effect of random variations in score, when the same test is administered a second time to a given group of pupils. The differences between scores on the two testing occasions will give the following distribution:

Figure 1: Distribution of score differences between two testing occasions (SE = standard error of test)

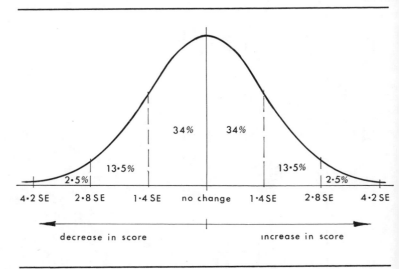

The reason why the standard deviation of this distribution is equal to 1.4 multiplied by the standard error of the test is beyond the scope of this book. (The correct value is actually SE X $\sqrt{2}$; the interested reader will find an explanation of this value in most elementary statistical texts.) However, it is reasonable for the error of the difference between two scores to be greater than the error of each individual score, since there are two errors involved in the difference.

Suppose that a class of pupils is assessed twice using a test with a standard error of three and the difference in score between the two testing occasions is found for each pupil. Reference to Figure 1 enables the following hypothetical distribution to be constructed (assuming no change in the attainment of the group):

Table 1

Change in score	*Percentage of pupils*
Gain of more than 8.4 points (2 x 1.4 x 3)	2.5%
Gain between 4.2 and 8.4 points	13.5%
Gain of less than 4.2 points (1.4 x 3)	34%
Loss of less than 4.2 points (1.4 x 3)	34%
Loss between 4.2 and 8.4 points	13.5%
Loss of more than 8.4 points (2 x 1.4 x 3)	2.5%

'No change' cases are shared equally by the two middle bands.

This distribution can be shown graphically as in Figure 2, thus providing a useful visual 'model' (representing the 'no-change' situation) which can be used as a yardstick to assess the extent of improvement in score from one occasion to the next.

Figure 2: Distribution of score differences between two testing occasions for a test of standard error 3 and no change in the attainment of the group.

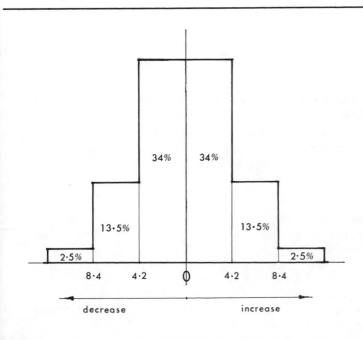

As an example, suppose there are 20 pupils in the class; the results might be as follows:

		score difference	
1st occasion	2nd occasion	increase	decrease
102	106	4	
100	98		2
103	98		5
99	96		3
90	101	11	
85	82		3
100	106	6	
120	123	3	
96	99	3	
104	96		8
70	71	1	
125	124		1
116	116	—	—
87	91	4	
101	100		1
99	101	2	
81	88	7	
110	107		3
98	97		1
102	102	—	—

To assess whether there has been any change in attainment, and if so in what direction, these results are tabulated in bands of 1.4 x SE, according to the distribution in Table 1 (Figure 2).

Change in score	Number and percentage of pupils	
Gain of more than 8.4 points	1	5%
Gain between 4.2 and 8.4 points	2	10%
Gain of less than 4.2 points	7	35%
Loss of less than 4.2 points	8	40%
Loss between 4.2 and 8.4 points	2	10%
Loss of more than 8.4 points	0	—

(The two cases where there has been no change are 'shared out' between the two central bands.)

These percentages can be plotted as a histogram on the same scale as the expected values and a direct comparison made:

Figure 3: Comparison between the expected and obtained distribution of score differences for the above hypothetical case.

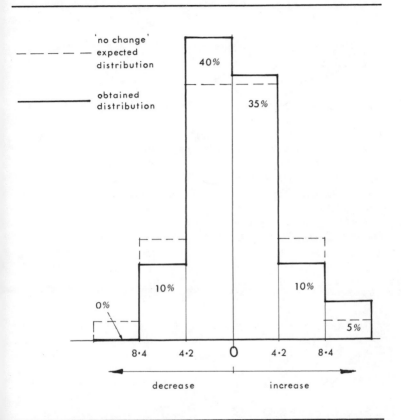

It can clearly be seen that there has been little change in the attainment of the group.

APPENDIX B: Other Tests Referred to in the Text

Auditory Discrimination Test, J.M. Wepman (1958), Chicago: Language Research Associates Inc.

Auditory Sequential Memory Test, J.M. Wepman & A. Morency (1973), Chicago: Language Research Associates Inc.

Coloured Progressive Matrices, R.C. Raven (1956), London: H.C. Lewis.

Durrell Analysis of Reading Difficulty, D.D. Durrell (1955), New York: Harcourt Brace and World, Inc.

English Picture Vocabulary Tests, A. Brimer and C.M. Dunn (1962), London: Nelson.

Harris Test of Lateral Dominance, A.J. Harris (1947), New York: The Psychological Corporation.

Illinois Test of Psycholinguistic Abilities, S.A. Kirk, J.J. McCarthy and W.D. Kirk (1968), Urbana: University of Illinois Press.

Non-Verbal Tests BD, D.A. Pidgeon (1964), Slough: NFER.

Non-Verbal Test DH, B. Calvert (1955), Slough: NFER.

Non-Reader's Intelligence Test, D. Young (1964), London: University of London Press.

Picture Intelligence Test A, J.E. Stuart (1954), Slough: NFER.

Progressive Matrices, J. Raven (1947), London: H.K. Lewis.

Visual Sequential Memory Tests, J.M. Wepman, A. Morency and M. Seid (1975), Chicago: Language Research Associates Inc.

APPENDIX C: TEST STATISTICS: Further Reading

A.C. Crocker, (1974) *Statistics for the Teacher*. Slough: NFER.
S. Jackson, (1971) *A Teacher's Guide to Testing*. London: Longmans.
W.H. King, (1969) *Statistics in Education*. London: Macmillan.
D.G. Lewis, (1967) *Statistical Methods in Education*. London: University of London Press.
D.M. Miller, (1972) *Interpreting Test Scores*. New York: John Wiley.
D. Pidgeon and A. Yates, (1968) *An Introduction to Educational Measurement*. London: Routledge and Kegan Paul.

APPENDIX D: Main Reading Test Publishers

Basil Blackwell and Mott Ltd., 108 Cowley Road, Oxford OX4 IJF.
Chatto and Windus Ltd., 40—42 William IV Street, London WC2N 4DF.
Evans Brothers Ltd., Montague House, Russell Square, London WC1B 5BX.
Robert Gibson and Sons Ltd., 17 Fitzroy Place, Glasgow.
George Harrap and Co. Ltd., 182 High Holborn, London WC1V 7AX.
Heinemann Educational Books Ltd., 48 Charles Street, Mayfair, London W1.
Macmillan and Co. Ltd., Brunel Road, Basingstoke, Hants.
NFER Publishing Co. Ltd., 2 Jennings Buildings, Thames Street, Windsor, Berks SL4 IQS.
Thomas Nelson and Sons, 36 Park Street, London W1.
Oliver and Boyd Ltd., Tweedale Court, 14 High Street, Edinburgh 1.
University of London Press Ltd., St. Paul's House, Warwick Lane, London EC4.

REFERENCES

BALLARD, P.B. (1960). *Mental Tests*. London: University of London Press.

BERSE, P. (1974). 'Criteria for the assessment of pupils' compositions', *Educational Research*, **17** 1, 54—61.

BORMOUTH, J.R. (1968). 'Cloze test readability: criterion-referenced scores', *J. Educ., Meas.* **5** 3, 189—95.

BYRNE, C.J. (1975). *Computerised Question Banking Systems*. Open University.

CLARKE, M.L. (1973). *Hierarchical Structure of Comprehension: Skills Volume 2*.Victoria: AGER.

CLAY, M.M. (1972a). *Reading: the Patterning of Complex Behaviour*. Auckland: Heinemann Educational Books.

CLAY, M.M. (1972b). *A Diagnostic Survey*. Auckland: Heinemann Educational Books.

CLYMER, T. (1972). 'What is reading?: some current concepts'. In: MELINK, A. and MERRIT, J. (Eds) *Reading Today and Tomorrow*. London: University of London Press.

CROCKER, A.C. (1974). *Statistics for the Teacher*. Slough: NFER.

DEAN, J. and NICHOLS, R. (1974). *Framework for Reading*. London: Evans.

DOWNING, J. and THACKRAY, D. (1971). *Reading Readiness*. London: University of London Press.

EDWARDS, R.P.A. and GIBBON, V. (1963). *Words Your Children Use*. London: Burke Publishing Company Ltd.

FARR, R. (1969). *Reading: What can be Measured?* Newark, Delaware: International Reading Association.

GASPAR, R. and BROWN, D. (1973). *Perceptual Processes in Reading*. London: Hutchinson Educational Ltd.

GILLILAND, J. (1973). *Readability*. London: University of London Press.

GOODMAN K.S. (Ed) (1968). *The Psycholinguistic Nature of the Reading Process*. Detroit: Wayne State University Press.

GOODMAN, Y. and BURKE, C. (1970). *Reading Miscues Inventory*. New York: Macmillan.

HARRIS, D.B. (1963). *Children's Drawings as a Measure of Intellectual Maturity*. New York: Harcourt, Brace and World.

HUGHES, J.M. (1975). *Reading and Reading Failures*. London: Evans.

HUNT, K.W. (1968). *An Instrument to Measure Syntactic Maturity, Preliminary Version*. Tallahassee, Florida State University (EDO 20926).

JACKSON, S. (1971). *Get Reading Right*. Glasgow: Gibson.

JOHNSON, M.S. and KRESS, R.A. (1965). *Informal Reading Inventories*. Newark, Delaware: International Reading Association.

KOHL, H. (1974). *Reading How To*. Harmondsworth: Penguin Books.

McNALLY, J. and MURRAY, W. (1964). *Keywords to Literacy*. London: Schoolmaster Publishing Co.

NEWCOMER, P.L. and HAMMILL, D.D. (1975). 'ITPA and academic achievement: a survey', *Reading Teacher*, May, 731–41.

NUTTALL, D.L. and SKURNIK, L.S. (1970). *Examinations and Item Analysis Manual*. Slough: NFER.

OPPENHEIM, A.N. (1966). *Questionnaire Design and Attitude Measurement*. London: Heinemann Educational Books.

PETERS, M. (1967). *Spelling: Caught or Taught?* London: Routledge and Kegan Paul.

PETERS, M. (1970). *Success in Spelling*. Cambridge: Cambridge University, Institute of Education.

POWELL, W.R. (1968). 'Criteria for interpreting Informal Reading Inventories'. In: DE BOER, D.L. (Ed) *Reading Diagnosis and Evaluation*. Newark, Delaware: International Reading Association.

REID, J. (1972). *Reading: Problems and Practices*. London: Ward Lock Educational.

STRANG, R. (1969). *The Diagnostic Teaching of Reading*. New York: McGraw Hill.

SULLIVAN, D.S. and HUMPHREY, J.H. (1973). *Teaching Reading Through Motor Learning*. Springfield, Illinois: Charles C. Thomas.

TANSLEY, A.E. (1967). *Reading and Remedial Reading*. London: Routledge and Kegan Paul.

VERNON, M.D. (1957). *Backwardness in Reading*. Cambridge: Cambridge University Press.

WILKINSON, A., STRATTA, L. and DUDLEY, P. (1974). *The Quality of Listening* and *Listening Comprehension Tests*. London: Macmillan.

COD. OE

The NFER Publishing Company's book publishing programme aims to make available new research findings and other original material of value to the educational world. The Company is associated with the National Foundation for Educational Research in England and Wales.

0 85633 101